401 (K)NO WLE DGE

J. Michael Scarborough
CEO, Scarborough Capital Management

Design: Love Has No Logic Design Group (lovehasnologic.com)
Creative Director: Mike Gibson

ISBN 978-0-87218-965-2

Library of Congress Control Number: 2008927261

1st Edition

Copyright © 2008
The National Underwriter Company
P.O. Box 14367, Cincinnati, Ohio 45250-0367

Printed in U. S. A.

Acknowledgments

I have spent the last 20 years of my life helping average Americans prudently plan for retirement by using their company-sponsored retirement plans wisely. It is a shared passion by everyone at Scarborough Capital Management. It is this passion for what we all do everyday that has made 401(k)nowledge possible. We can only hope that this passion is infectious and everyone who entrusts us with their financial future feels this passion as well.

There are several people who I have the pleasure of working with everyday who have made this book possible.

I need to recognize the outstanding contributions of the entire Scarborough Capital Management team. Their professionalism and high level of client service has made Scarborough Capital Management a company synonymous with the 401(k) marketplace. Thank you to you all.

The book would not exist without the belief that Debbie Miner and her team at National Underwriter have in me and the concept for the book. I am thrilled they saw the value in a book on how people used their 401(k) plans to retire successfully. Also, I need to acknowledge the efforts of designer extraordinaire, Michael Gibson, my publicist and friend, Ben Lewis of Perception, Inc., and Steven Jones-D'Agostino, who helped me transform my thoughts and "401(k)nowledge" into the book you have in your hands.

Finally, I need to thank my kids, Katherine and Matthew. They are the inspiration for everything I do in life. Without their love and support, I would not be where I am today.

Table of Contents

Prologue

Who I am, why I wrote this book, and what I hope you will get from it.

I believe passionately that the 401(k) is *the* tool that determines how well or poorly we will live in retirement. I also realize, however, that most of us lack the skills and abilities to use this tool in a proper and effective way.

I have been in the retirement-planning business for 25 years. In 1984, when I worked for Dean Witter in Cherry Hill, New Jersey, I met with some employees of a local plant of Mobil (now Exxon Mobil). They asked me to explain their 401(k)s to them. They did not understand their plans, had a fair amount of money in them, and needed help managing their portfolios. It took me a while to understand the depth and breadth of their problem. However, the more I worked with them, the more I realized how little they knew about their 401(k)s.

One of the truisms of the investment industry is: "If you do not pay financial planners to advise you, they would have no incentive to really help you." With this in mind, I recognized a blind spot in the marketplace. Across America, millions of people had saved and invested sizeable chunks of money for their retirements, yet they often did not receive sound advice from professionals with a financial stake to help them achieve their goals. Back then, many people thought their employers looked out for them regarding their 401(k)s. They were wrong. When it comes to company retirement plans, employers need to look out for their own financial interests, not those of their employees.

During the last 23 years, I have largely seen this sad scenario disappear. This said, I continue to meet people who think wrongly that the financial manager hired by their company to run the firm's 401(k) plan is also managing their own money. They think these managers will successfully guide them to a comfortable retirement. Most of the retirement-planning lessons I have learned well have been the result of mistakes I have made or seen others make. Therefore, I have profiled 20 Scarborough clients and non-clients for this book as a viable way to share practical "401(k)nowledge" with you. Working together, we can create a groundswell for retiring on *our* terms.

Hopefully, you will finish this book with the sense that you alone possess the ability to control your retirement destiny. You do not need to be saving and investing at the market's whim. My hope is to convert all of you, one reader at a time, to this way of thinking. I aspire to take what we do for a living at Scarborough Capital Management and make it an integral part of the corporate world's social fabric. The social implications are huge and profound.

If you follow my practical 401(k) advice, you could continue affording health insurance and medical care when you retire. In doing so, you also could continue avoiding the stigma of being a burden on our state and federal governments.

J. Michael Scarborough
CEO, Scarborough Capital Management

Foreword

By Ted Benna

Father of the 401(k)
Savings Plan and COO
Malvern Benefits
Corporation

I entered the retirement business more than 48 years ago as an actuarial clerk in the home office of an insurance company. My primary experience has involved helping employers establish and successfully operate all types of retirement programs. Employers become involved with retirement programs to help them attract and retain good employees but to also help their employees prepare for retirement. Although most of my experience is at the corporate level, I have also had considerable contact with employees who are participants in such plans. At the age of 66, I am also able to relate to the stages of retirement that Mike covers in this book. I have learned much about this subject from others over the years and I have also learned a great deal on my own.

I have seen dramatic changes in this field during the years that I have been engaged in this business. Probably the most significant change is the shift from corporate to individual responsibility. The first big employer I helped introduce to a 401(k) savings plan was Bethlehem Steel during early 1981. I stated, during my first meeting with members of senior management, that it was time for their employees to start saving for retirement. I was politely told that Bethlehem Steel employees didn't need to do this because the company took care of its employees forever. How things have changed!!

I am often asked by members of the media whether it was my intent to see employer-funded defined benefit plans replaced by 401(k) plans. The answer is no. Savings plans like 401(k) were intended to add to Social Security and employer-funded retirement benefits. But many larger employers have dropped pension benefits and the number doing so is growing rapidly. As a result, very few private sector non-bargaining workers entering the workplace are receiving pension benefits. Virtually all will have to build their retirement benefits through defined contribution plans like 401(k) where each employee must assume the responsibility for knowing how much to contribute and how to invest the money. It should be noted that this shift of responsibility from corporate to the individual would have occurred even if 401(k) never existed. The reasons behind this shift are too complex to cover in this brief introduction. If it is of interest to you, go to malvern401k.net for a detailed explanation of the history of 401(k) and this shift. Click on history, then at the end of the two page "cliff notes" version there is a place where you can click for a much more detailed explanation.

In any event, this shift has happened – and it isn't going to change – so you need to face this reality. It is your responsibility to plan for your retirement. You can't count on someone else to do it for you. Members of the media have also often asked me what are the biggest mistakes people make regarding planning for retirement. I tell them at the top of the list is failing to plan for retirement. Retirement planning is one of the major life events requiring careful planning over many years. Attempting to make the trip without a plan is similar to putting a 16 year old in a car in New York City and telling him/her to drive to San Diego without using a map or any road signs. There is some small chance he/she will eventually reach the Pacific Ocean but probably far off the San Diego target.

Learning from others is a great way to help you develop a retirement plan if you don't have one or to refine the one you do have. The examples Mike uses is this book are real people who have a similar goal to yours – successfully retiring. Learn from their experiences.

At age 66, my own planning still involves stages similar to what Mike suggests in this book. I am semi-retired at this point. My goal between now and age 70 is to earn a sufficient amount that I don't have to touch my retirement savings or other assets. I am blessed with good fortune and health that enables me to earn what I need without working a lot of hours. The next stage is likely to be a further reduction in working time. I expect to tap into my retirement savings at that point. The third stage, if my wife or I are still living, is post age 85. We have specific assets set aside for that period of life if needed as protection against increased health care costs or other needs.

I was involved two months ago in conducing educational meetings for employees at a specific company. The major focus of these meetings dealt with investing because I was helping this employer totally restructure its retirement program. One of the employees told me after one of the meetings that he and the other employees would have paid more attention if I told them I made lots of money, retired, and was now telling them how to do it. So, I told employees during the remaining meetings that financially I could have retired at age 49 but didn't. I entered the "work force" at age 6 on our family's dairy farm. I currently enjoy biking, running, walking in the mountains, home construction projects and especially spending time with our family members including nine grandchildren. But I am not at a point where a life that involves only leisure activities is likely to be fulfilling. Our Creator didn't intend for us to be inactive half of our adult lives. As a result, as Mike's book notes, retirement planning involves both financial and non-financial issues. Both are of equal importance.

Will you stay in your current area when you retire? Will you downsize your home? How will you spend your time? My wife and I tackled the first of these issues during our mid fifties by moving from suburban Philadelphia to north Central PA where the cost of living is lower and the pace of life is less stressful. We selected this location because it is close to part of our family and it is similar to the rural area where we both grew up. It is best to begin considering these non-financial issues at least a couple of years before you plan to retire. The cooperation of your spouse is obviously essential if you have one.

An extremely important point is that the sooner you start planning for retirement the more likely you are to be successful. Perhaps an equally important point is the fact that failing will be painful. You won't have the chance to learn from your failed experience and do it over. This reminds me of the fact that I failed one of my college math classes when I took the course during the summer when I didn't have enough time to deal with such a complex course over a shortened semester. I was able to successfully complete this class when I took it over during the next semester. You can't do that with retirement planning. This is why it is so important to use this book and other resources to develop a retirement plan and then track your progress toward your goal. Remember, you can't count on someone else to do this for you – it is your responsibility.

Profiles

Let me introduce you to the people I interviewed for this book.

I am extremely grateful to the 10 Scarborough Capital Management clients and the 10 non-clients who have shared their "401(k) nowledge" with me. In turn, I share their valuable gift with you. They are listed here in alphabetical order by first name. In exchange for their generous cooperation, I have agreed not to reveal their last names.

Andrew, 28, has worked for Cardinal Health and invested in its 401(k) plan for nearly four years. Previously, he was employed by National City Bank. Armed with an undergraduate degree in business administration and working toward an MBA, he manages his own 401(k) plan. He is not a client of Scarborough Capital Management.

Ann, 37, is an attorney for a prominent law firm and invests in its 401(k) plan. She expects to nearly double her retirement fund by the time she is 40. Right now, at least, she has no problem working until she is 70. She hopes to live to 120. She is not a client of ours.

Barbara, 62, has worked more than 37 years for a unit of Northrop Grumman, which was a unit of Westinghouse when she joined the company. She plans to retire in the next year or two, once she and her husband retire the mortgages on their two homes. We do not manage her retirement fund.

Bob, 58, retired in 2000 while working for Lucent Technologies. In 1968, he started his career with the Bell System at New York Telephone. Subsequently, he transferred to Southwestern Bell and then moved to AT&T when Bell spun off its Regional Bell Operating Companies (RBOCs) in 1984. He finished his 35-year telecommunications career at Avaya, which AT&T divested in 1996. He worked for Avaya for three years after his official retirement. He is a Scarborough Capital Management client.

Carol, 51, worked for AT&T for most of her career and now works for a private telecommunications company. She has saved and invested retirement money since she was 27. We manage her 401(k) plan.

Carrie, 24, is a recent college graduate who majored in writing. She works in marketing and public relations at a company in the Northeast. She is eligible to join her company's 401(k) but has yet to do so. She is not a client of ours.

Dick, 60, has worked for General Motors or "The General," as he calls it, since 1967. He joined the company's retirement plan five years later. He had hoped to work until he was 62. Instead, he accepted a generous, early retirement package from "The General" in 2006. We manage his retirement portfolio.

Dixie, 68, is a legal secretary for a prominent law firm and invests in its 401(k) plan. Her husband is retired and collecting Social Security. He does not have either a pension or a 401(k) plan. We do not manage her retirement fund.

Gary, 53, was a General Motors (GM) employee from 1975 to 1996. Since his first GM paycheck, he participated in the company's stock-savings plan. In 1986, he joined GM's 401(k) plan upon becoming a salaried employee. Ten years later, he left GM to take an ownership stake and management job at a class-8 new truck dealership. He takes part in the dealership's 401(k) plan and has a Roth IRA, which he began before joining the dealership. The Scarborough Capital Management manages his retirement funds.

Greg, 61, has worked for GM since 1973. He hopes to retire in two years. He hires us to manage his retirement funds.

Jennifer, 28, has been an attorney for a prominent law firm for one year. Each month, she makes a good effort to invest the maximum allowable amount in the firm's 401(k) plan. Since she was 18, she has saved and invested with help from a professional financial advisor. She is not a Scarborough Capital Management client.

John, 64, retired in 2001 as a long-time employee of GM. He joined GM in 1965 as an industrial engineer right after graduating from college with a major in industrial engineering and minors in economics and philosophy. We manage his retirement portfolio.

Kim, 50, has worked her entire 28-year career for the Bell System, first for AT&T, then for Lucent Technologies and now for Avaya. She has a 401(k) and other retirement investments and plans to retire within three years. She has been a Scarborough Capital Management client for more than 20 years.

Lou, 61, retired in 2006 while employed at AT&T. He began working for the Bell System in 1969. Fifteen years later, he went to work for AT&T when Bell spun off its RBOCs. He is a client of ours.

Neil, 56, began working for GM as a student in training in 1977. He became a full-time GM employee three years later. He married in 1987 and divorced in 2000. Because he lacked a prenuptial agreement, he spent a year and significant legal fees to reach a divorce settlement with his former wife. As a result, he reduced significantly his 401(k) contributions. In 2006, he received a large pay raise from GM. Sometime in 2007, he hopes to resume the maximum allowable contribution to his 401(k). We manage his retirement portfolio.

Omar, 34, has worked for the U.S. Treasury for nearly four years. Most of his 401(k) is in stocks and the rest, in Treasury notes. He also has a Roth IRA, which he plans to use to buy a house. In October 2007, he will leave his government post for a job in the private sector. His new employer's 401(k) plan provides many more investment options than the federal government's plan. In addition, the company has a profit-sharing plan. We do not manage Omar's retirement funds.

Ron, 60, is a long-time AT&T employee who now works for American Systems. He took part in AT&T's retirement plan but does not participate in American Systems' 401(k) plan. He draws a pension from Lucent Technologies, which was spun off by AT&T in 1996 and merged with Alcatel 10 years later. The Scarborough Capital Management manages his retirement plan.

Stephanie, 40, has worked for General Motors Assistance Corporation for 18 years. For 17 of them, she has contributed to her company's 401(k) plan. She hopes to retire at 65 and live to 105. We manage her retirement portfolio.

Valerie, 32, participates in her company's 401(k) plan. She has a significant portion of her retirement money invested in risky holdings, which is fine. She will need to reduce this risk, however, once she is much closer to retirement. She is not a client of ours.

Wendy, 35, works for a real-estate investment trust. She and her husband are expecting their first child. Conceivably, she could leave the workplace for several years to raise children. We do not manage her 401(k) plan.

1

What Does Planning for and Living in Retirement Mean to You?

Most people outlive their money supply.

Good news: You're going to live forever! Alright, that was meant to get your attention. But, if you're going to have a full, secure retirement, you should handle your finances as if you were going to live to be 1,000.

As I noted in *The Scarborough Plan: Maximizing the Power of Your 401(k)*, retirement begins when you cease relying on your company, business, or organization to figure out for you how you will spend your days. Sometimes, you have the pleasure of deciding when that happens. Other times, higher powers determine the fate of your future. Regardless of how it happens, when you retire, you are no longer working at the job you have loved, hated, or merely tolerated for longer than you can remember.

What happens next depends upon what you want to – or must – do based largely on how well you have planned up to that point. Three basic stages of retirement face you, and you may end up passing through any or all of them before you graduate from retirement to, well, death.

Stage One is for those of you who continue to work – part-time or full-time – after you retire. Many people begin second careers, turn their hobbies into income-producing businesses, or simply enjoy the social interactions they get from working at a job that is quite different from their previous one. The point is that many people still work in some capacity during their early retirement. The work provides some income, so they have less need to dip into whatever assets they accumulated during their *real* working life.

Stage Two pertains to those of you who have finished working – *really* finished working. No more hawking your jewelry at crafts shows, no more consulting, no more "would you like fries with that?" Because of judicious spending and, with any luck, accumulating some valuable assets – that five-bedroom house, for example – you do not need to tap those still-growing retirement resources. Instead, you can use some of your cash reserves that are not earning much income, sell the house and live off some of the proceeds while investing the rest, and auction that Andy Warhol painting you never liked anyway.

Stage Three is the one you eventually want to reach. You may have liquidated all the assets you want to liquidate. You may have drawn down your cash reserves to a level below which you would be comfortable. Or you may have reached the second legal age of your life – the one when you *must* begin withdrawing from one or all of your retirement accounts. At this point, you will be fully reliant on the income created by the assets you accumulated in all the prior years. Your retirement planning does not end at this point. You must still be able to implement a strategy of withdrawal that maximizes your cash flow, minimizes your taxes and maintains – as far as possible – the principal amounts in your retirement accounts.

Stage three – and when you plan to reach it – is the most critical of the three. You need to know when you will require your retirement monies because the amount of time between now and then determines everything – from how much you need to set aside regularly, to how you invest what you do set aside. Starting now is critically important. The dollar you invest today is worth more than the dollar you invest tomorrow. The sooner you begin to save and invest for retirement, the longer you will have to contribute to your plan and watch it grow before you reach this stage of your life in retirement.

Experience shows us that 97 percent of retired people have a lifestyle well *below* that when they worked full time. The reason is simple: Many people fail to plan well for their retirement. This is especially true of many employees at big, financially troubled companies such as General Motors. Their contributions to the company retirement plan have dried up because of the huge legacy costs their company has to shoulder.

My advice is take no more than 4.5 percent a year from your 401(k) or other retirement plan for living and other expenses. In recent years, the annual inflation rate has averaged 2.5 percent. Therefore, when you take 4.5 percent annually from your plan, your investment adviser needs to make your money grow at least 7 percent a year just to keep your plan from shrinking.

Many people also make a big mistake when they believe they will remain alive only 20 or so years in retirement. Given continual advances in medical and health care, you will probably live much longer than you think. Yet another error many people commit is to presume they will stay healthy during all of their retirement years. They need to be like Stephanie and Barbara.

Stephanie presumes she is going to live *forever* and manages her money accordingly. This way, when she dies *before* forever – as all of us will certainly do – she will *not* have outlived her money. As for Barbara, both of her parents are in their late 80s, causing her to she hope she will have a long, healthy life. This also leads her to realize she cannot spend all of her money in the first few years of retirement.

Regardless of how you define retirement, you need to become comfortable with the idea of retiring. Greg has finally achieved this state of mind. For many years, though, he considered retirement to be either something other people did or a theoretical notion. You might ask yourself, "Why can't I spend my money to enjoy life while I can?" This could be an option, unless you plan to leave a significant amount of your estate to your heirs.

Ideally, Carol would like to leave *something* to her stepchildren. However, they earn more than she does – at least, right now – so she does not worry about them. Instead, she plans to live in retirement as though she *could* spend her last dollar.

This is the attitude I urged one previous client to adopt. She was terminally ill and had two sons. One was 17 and the other, 19. The three of them had always wanted to go on a long vacation sea cruise. However, the mother had yet to arrange for the journey because she was still shopping around for the most inexpensive airfares. This, even though she had several hundred thousand dollars in savings. Bluntly, I told her, "You're out of your mind! I'm going to book the airline tickets for you and your boys. It's not going to matter how much they cost, and you're going to go on this cruise." She and her sons took the cruise, and she died only six weeks after returning.

Whether or not you are terminally ill, you should not spend all your retirement money all at once. However, you should live fully and within reasonable boundaries while you are alive.

Light Years Away

Valerie, 32, views retirement as being light years away – especially Stage Three. Like many people in her age group, she expects to live, she says kiddingly, *"forever!"* Becoming serious, she says she will retire between the ages of 60 and 65 and live another 20 to 25 years. This presumes, of course, that she remains healthy and well in retirement. Fair enough.

However, what would she do with all her time? "I'm close to my family, so I would spend a lot of time with them. I'd also like to travel," she answers. "I don't know what else I'd be into doing then. It's so far away." Valerie, who is not our client, does have a general idea of what she wants from life in retirement. "Hopefully, I will have enough money saved so that I don't have to work and I can still do the things I enjoy doing," she says.

Her sense of retirement is quite normal for someone her age. To her and other young people at or near the beginning of their work careers, I offer three pieces of advice:

1. Start saving enough money for retirement once you get out of school. Keep in mind that saving for retirement is something that should be done over a lifetime. There are no Get Rich Quick schemes when it comes to retirement, only Get Rich Slowly schemes.

2. Continue to save and plan enough to achieve your retirement goal. You need to save consistent amounts during your work-

ing years, and you have to know what that amount should be in order to meet your goals. Toward that end you need to …

3. Have a methodology to realize your retirement plan.

A Lot of Living to Do

Valerie can learn much from Stephanie, who hopes to live to a healthy 105. Stephanie, 40, plans to retire at 65. She plans to have "a lot of living to do" in retirement.

She has contributed to her company-sponsored 401(k) plan for 17 of her 18 years at GMAC. At the beginning of her employment there, she set aside a small amount from each paycheck – 6 percent – to her plan because she was earning only $1,750 a month, and most of that was paying for basic living expenses. Now, she averages about 8 percent a paycheck – at times, as high as 10 percent – on a much larger salary.

However, she lacks a financial plan to support her longevity goal, and she has yet to inform her financial adviser of the goal. "I probably need to let him know that the next time we talk!" she says. She thinks this information "might very well" be useful to her adviser. "He needs all of the information so he can make the best choices and decisions for me," she says. She expects her adviser "to laugh" good naturedly when she informs him of her longevity goal.

Even if Stephanie never works a paying job once she retires, the money in her retirement account would need to continue growing. Otherwise, she could eat into the principal amount well before she reaches 105. "That's *not* want I want! – that's *not* optimal!" she says. "If I die and my money is still around, that's *great*." She does not plan to spend "every last dime" of her retirement money before she dies. "But it'd be nice to have the *option* to do that," she says.

Stephanie, who was a finance major in college, has a clear vision of her life in retirement. She also possesses a good, general understanding of how money works, calling herself "an informed consumer." She attributes this healthy awareness to her good upbringing. Her parents worked and saved to, among other things, put their three daughters through college and see two of them get married. They also live comfortably and travel a lot. "I think they managed their money pretty well," she says. She picked up this trait from observing her parents. "It's not what's said [that causes us to learn]," she says. "It's what's *heard*."

Stephanie, who is single, realizes fully that she needs to take good financial care of herself. "I need to make sure I'm doing the *best* and the *most* I can in order to do that," she says. She views her financial independence as one of the biggest gifts she can give to her parents. Having it, she tells her parents to spend all of their money while they are alive. "Don't leave a cent behind," she says. "I'm okay and my sisters are okay. So spend your money! Travel! Go enjoy life! You spent all those years raising us. Now, it's time for you to go have fun *again*."

Some of our clients frighten me when they say they intend to fund their retirement with an *inheritance* from their parents. At the risk of being a bit morbid, you have no idea if your parents will prede-cease you. And, it seems to me, building your retirement plans around a positive financial outcome from your parents' death colors you parent/child relationship with a pretty dark brush.

Stephanie has a wonderful vision of her life in retirement. She is "living in a very comfortable atmosphere – preferably, on the water – and not having to worry or be concerned about paying my bills." Not that she plans to stop working altogether. She just does not want to *need* to work. "[I may] want to be the greeter at Wal-Mart because I just want to greet people," she says.

An increasing number of retired Americans work as greeters and baggers at Wal-Mart and other big-chain stores and supermarkets. The Social Security Administration estimates that 29 percent of retired people's money comes from paid jobs. For the most part, this is not because they *want* to work. Instead, it is because they need to pay their bills.

As Stephanie relates, "I was in CVS [pharmacy] the other day and I saw this Asian lady who is probably as old as my grandmother. "I said to myself, 'Holy [heck]! I certainly don't want to have to work at CVS to make ends meet.' I will do that, if necessary, because I'm not afraid of working. But it will be really nice not to have to."

Do not look for Stephanie to become a reclusive retiree, though. "One of the biggest things about growing old is that you have to keep your mind active," she says. "Some people work at places like Wal-Mart just to keep their mind active and their social skills honed so they're not sitting like lumps in front of the TV all day."

A Long, Comfortable Retirement

To hear Barbara, 61, tell her husband's and her story, they are in for a long, comfortable retirement. This is because they have done an excellent job preparing themselves for this stage of their lives. Barbara, at least, also has a good, healthy attitude about life in retirement.

She and her husband live most of the time in an upscale, golf-course community in Maryland and own a second home in Florida. They bought their Maryland home about 12 years ago for less than $200,000, putting quite a bit down just as the real estate market there started to bloom. These days, their outstanding mortgage is less than $100,000 at a time when prices for homes there start in the $400,000s. Eventually, they want to retire to Florida without needing to work a paying job. "If I get bored, don't have enough interests and want to go back to work, that would be fine," she says. "But I don't really want to have to do that."

When Barbara entered the workforce 38 years ago, she had no clue what life in retirement meant. To her, it was an abstract notion. "I was in my early 20s and was single," she says. "The last thing on my mind was retirement. I was too stupid to get in a [retirement] or savings plan until pretty close to 10 years into my employment here" at the company where she then and now works.

The company where Barbara works has a match plan. She regards her participation tardiness as "probably the biggest" mistake she has made. She remembers thinking, in her 20s, she would eventually marry a man who would "take care of her" so she would not need to work when she reached her current age. She also recalls *not* thinking, "There are two of us. Wouldn't it be better to have two of us saving?"

In fairness to Barbara, this mindset was quite typical of married couples decades ago. These days, she recommends – as I do – that young, married couples invest immediately in a retirement plan. All we have to do is look at the high divorce rates in this country to understand why everyone should plan for his/her own retirement. And, even if your marriage remains healthy, you'll build a better joint retirement if you are both working to achieve financial goals.

Barbara's goal is to retire in the next year or two. First, though, she and her husband need to pay off the mortgages on their two homes, which they are close to retiring. "That's one reason I haven't retired before this," she says. "Also, both my parents are still alive, and I'm an only child. They live [nearby] and I can't just take off and do whatever I want."

She has a good general sense of what life in retirement will be for her. However, she also is hard-pressed to say how long she thinks she will live. "It'd be pretty nice to be comfortable and flexible in what I can and can't do," she says. "But, no, I'm not going to say, 'I've got just a short time left to live. Let's blow it all until there's nothing left.'"

As with Stephanie, Barbara will not sit around the house in retirement. She is witnessing first-hand the impact of this sort of behavior on her husband, who retired four years ago. "Frankly, he's been bored," she says. "He's home alone a lot, and he doesn't play golf or any kind of thing like that. Many of his friends are also retired, so he has been doing a little pick-up work on the side just to have something to do. That way, he's not sitting in the house day after day reading a book."

Her husband has not worked a paying job in retirement because they did not need the extra money. When his mother died a few years ago, his brother and he inherited a significant amount of money. His brother used his own share to buy their mother's house. Barbara's husband invested his own share, and when he retired, cashed out in a lump sum. "So we've got some money put away," she says. While she admits to be more of a spender than her husband is, she says they are in good financial shape and do not have many credit-card bills to pay.

Barbara is fully aware that once she retires, her investments can continue to grow in size. In fact, her husband and she have not touched any of the money in his retirement account.

Eventually, they plan to sell their primary home in Maryland. They also intend to pay off the mortgage on their second home in Florida, which she and her husband own on a 50/50 basis with her parents, and move there. In addition, they look to live off the rest of the cash – around $300,000 – they expect to realize from the sale of their primary home. "That would cover us for a *long* time," she says.

Pleasure traveling is one of the activities Barbara and her husband plan to do more of, once she retires. But do not expect to see them go on extravagant trips to London, Paris or Madrid, though. If anything, they expect to maintain the lifestyle to which they have become accustomed.

I hope Barbara and her husband actually achieve their goal as well as avoid long, costly health problems. If they do, they should live comfortably for a long time to come.

Crossing the Rubicon

Greg crossed a Rubicon in 2006 regarding retirement. "Now, it's for real on the horizon," he says. He plans to retire in five years, when he turns 65, although he intends to keep active. "And not as the greeter at Wal-Mart, either!" he says. In five years, he will pay off his home mortgage as long as he continues making the same monthly payments as now. Then, he plans to use the home's equity to enjoy some of the luxuries of life.

He wonders whether he should completely retire – that is, not hold a paying job at all. "I don't have fears of retirement, although there's a degree of concern about the unknown," he says. "I think there's an adjustment period that my wife and I are going through right now. " He wants to save enough money so he does not have to work another day in his life once he does retire. "That said, I know I'm going to do something to keep busy once I retire," he says.

Greg and his wife, who is two years younger than he is, have discussed doing volunteer work in retirement. However, she may continue working for several more years – beyond when he plans to retire. "We're doing well, and we need to do something for other people," he says. "But if I'm going to work where there's any kind of stress, I'm going to want to get paid." They also plan to establish and maintain a principal amount in their retirement fund that will last "for some foreseeable future," he says. Their goal is to live off the interest. "I want to keep the money working," he says. "God forbid, something happens like a storm blowing away the house."

He advises young people who are just beginning to invest in a retirement fund to realize it is a learning process. "Over the years, light bulbs went on in my head, so to speak," he says. "I don't think I could have had this conversation about investment advice when I was 21." Now, he has more money than he ever dreamed possible. "Maybe my inactiveness on my investments at times was a kind of insulating factor," he says.

Greg recalls employees in the GM marketing center back in '86 checking the stock market online. "I thought to myself, 'these guys are screwed up somehow. It's like they're running from pillar to post. If they're successful, God bless them,'" he says. He continues to resist the urge to be reactionary. He also tries not to get excited when the market swings wildly. "I always tell my kids, 'the first thing you do when things go wrong is, don't panic.'"

Prior to September 11, 2001, Greg recalls looking at the healthy amount of money in his investment plan and saying to his wife, "I can't believe it's true." Then, the terrorists struck and the stock market crashed. His reaction: "Okay, let's not panic." His investment fund has fully recovered from the effects of 9/11. "At times, procrastination pays!" he says. (I will deal more with this topic in Chapter 7, titled *Do Not Panic When the Value of Your Plan Declines.*)

Greg has a healthy long-term view of his retirement savings. He understood that, as horrific as an event as 9/11 was – politically, socially, AND economically – it made no sense to let it dominate his thinking in terms of his retirement planning. We really should avoid knee-jerk jerk reactions, even to monumental events.

Not Working At All

While Greg may want to work part-time once he retires, Carol will have none of that. She defines "retirement" as *not working at all.* She would like to be able to retire and collect Social Security in 11 years, when she turns 62. However, she thinks this will not happen until she is at least 66. "Lately, I think more and more about retirement – and, I'll be honest with you, I get more and more greedy," she says.

Carol considers the fact she will have much more in savings at age 66 than at age 62. She will also be able to draw more from Social Security at 66 than 62. "It entices me more and more to work until I'm 66," she says. She hopes to use her retirement money primarily to travel abroad at least once a year and have a vacation home nearby. She plans to pay off her home mortgage in 10 years and continue living in her house once she retires. "My goal would be to really spend almost down to a bare minimum while I'm still alive," she says. "I feel that if I am going to work all those years, I'm entitled to spend that money."

That said, do not expect her to act foolishly with her retirement money. "Security is very important to me," she says. "I would be mortified if I ever had to borrow from my stepchildren. That would kill me." If anything, she wants to be in a position where she can donate some of her retirement money to charity. Another of her goals is to live at least until her mid 80s. "If I could live until I'm 84, I'd be real happy," she says. What if she is destined to live to *94?* "That means I'd better work until I'm 70!" she responds.

Carol has consistently saved money all her life. I suspect this is not going to change much between now and when she does retire. I feel she will continue to save money even in retirement. I bet she never spends her last dollar. Indeed, I wager she does not come close.

Saving is a habit that will serve you well – both in your accumulation and consumption years. If you continue to save – even after you retire – you can be sure of a secure retirement.

A Pretty Good Grip

Kim, 50, of Avaya has been quite good at saving money since she first began working for the Bell System. She has yet to borrow from her 401(k) plan. Before she hired us more than 20 years ago to manage her money, she had an opportunity to diversify her retirement portfolio. She grabbed it and did quite well. Now, she plans to retire within three years. To her, retirement means not working full-time for Avaya – or anyone else.

Will she work at least part-time in retirement? "It depends how my financial advisor does for me!" she responds only somewhat in jest. She goes on to say, "I actually think I could live off what I have in my 401(k) and in my other retirement investments. I would not necessarily have to work, but I might also have to watch a little more closely what I spend, when I travel, and what I do with the second half of my life."

Kim considers herself lucky that when she first went to work in the Bell System, specifically for AT&T, the company offered its employees a long-term savings plan. However, the plan contained only AT&T stock. "In those days, Ma Bell was mom and apple pie, and there forever – very stable," she says. "So I looked at it as a good investment."

Kim began to invest in the plan as soon as she joined AT&T. "Basically, that's what started my savings for retirement," she says. When AT&T began offering a 401(k) plan, it expanded the offerings to other investment options as well. Under both plans, AT&T also provided guaranteed matching funds of 4 percent of an employee's annual salary to employees who invested at least 6 percent of their annual salary. "To me, a 4 percent return was a pretty good guarantee," she says. "So I started from the get-go maxing out that savings plan."

When she began working for AT&T, the maximum amount an employee could put in the savings plan was around 15 percent of his or her annual salary. The company matched the first 6 percent. For a while, when her company was known as Lucent, it reduced somewhat its match to the 401(k) plan. The company became Avaya in 2000, and by 2003 it returned the match to 4 percent. However, Avaya eliminated its contribution to the employee pension plan. While Kim remains eligible for a pension, it is frozen at the 2003 level.

When Kim first began working for AT&T, she also contributed on a pre-tax basis to an AT&T-offered Individual Retirement Account (IRA). "Pre-tax, you basically got a little more for your money because you didn't pay taxes on it," she says. "So basically it was to encourage you to save." Twenty-eight years ago, she focused primarily on saving money for purposes other than retirement. "I thought I could retire on my pension," she says. These days, she cannot afford to retire on her pension alone.

A quarter century ago, Kim's thinking was sound. Many employees thought likewise. This was before too many companies either eliminated their contributions to pension plans, or outright raided the plans. Managing money may not be Kim's professional forte.

Nevertheless, she has intuitively known when to move away from higher-risk investments such at AT&T, Lucent and now Avaya. In this respect, she has a good grip on saving and investing for her retirement.

CHAPTER 1 401(K)NOWLEDGE GAINS

- Identify and aim for the stage in which you want to enter retirement.
- Start saving enough money for this stage of retirement once you leave school and enter the full-time workforce.
- Continue to save and plan enough to achieve your retirement goal.
- Establish and follow a methodology to realize your retirement plan.
- Take no more than 4.5 percent a year from your 401(k) or other retirement plan for living and other expenses because you may live much longer than you think.
- Do not presume you will stay healthy during all of your retirement years.
- Even if you are quite ill in retirement, live fully and within reasonable boundaries while you *are* alive.

2

Participate Actively in the Makeup of Your 401(k) Plan

Do not be an ostrich.

Avoid at all costs the "ostrich" method of investing. You know: Stick your head in the sand and hope that when you pull it out, enough money awaits you in retirement. Far more people do this than you might realize.

We have thousands of clients. Not all of them are ostriches, of course. However, the classic clients with their heads in the sand possess these traits:

- Have only about $50,000 in their 401(k) plan.
- Are in their mid- to late 50s.
- Want us to manage their money in an aggressive, growth way.
- Think they are being aggressive by saving only 10% of their income a year.
- Assume their portfolios will augment their pension and maintain the lifestyle to which they have become accustomed, once they retire.

Another big mistake many people make is to regard other people as smarter than themselves regarding investments. Too often, the other people are not. Sholmo Berartzi, a UCLA professor and one of the top behavioral finance people in the world, likes to tell of the sushi chef for the Biltmore Hotel in downtown Los Angeles. All of the Japanese restaurant workers including the sushi chef were saving money for retirement. All the chef's Japanese co-workers concluded he was the smartest among them because he spoke English as well as Japanese. Therefore, they assumed he was correctly handling his 401(k) plan. He was not. Still, like lemmings to the sea, they followed his investment strategy right over the edge of the cliff.

You can learn well from the stories of three ostriches, Bob, Neil, and Dick. They are examples of the worst that can possibly happen when you invest your money in only one stock and watch idly as it takes a beating. This sort of financial calamity occurs when you fail to participate actively in the makeup your 401(k) plan. Of course, we cannot legislate intelligence. We can recognize, however, that simply putting money in our 401(k) plan is not the same as participating actively in the plan. Active participation equals fiduciary responsibility.

In *The Scarborough Plan: Maximizing the Power of Your 401(k)*, I emphasized that the best retirement plan in the world will fail unless you actively follow and participate in the plan. I have met people who have paid hundreds of dollars to financial planners or retirement counselors for the best plans money can buy. Then these people do nothing with the plans. They nod their heads, take the personalized plans home and lose them in a stack of magazines. I know this sounds crazy but you will find people who do not follow through – at all!

Nearly as bad as no execution is poor execution. You get started down the right road to retirement but are sidetracked somewhere along the way. Maybe you do not understand the concepts under-lying a good retirement plan (which both of these books will fix). Maybe your investments performed poorly for one quarter and you lost confidence and moved them around without giving realloca-tion the same careful consideration you gave the original allocation. Maybe you simply do not pay any attention to your plan – ever – and have total disregard for what is happening in the financial markets and in the economy. Or maybe you have gotten weary of participating actively in the make-up of your plan. Sticking with your plan is not easy when you are bombarded with the prom-ise of "100 percent returns in six months – guaranteed!" If it gives you any comfort, you are not alone. Most people fall short of their retirement-plan goals because of poor execution, not poor planning.

Here are three steps you need to follow in order to reach that rich retirement you seek.

1. Make a good, realistic plan – one that will give you the best possible growth for your personal risk tolerance. Both of these books will play a key role in your active financial planning for retirement.

2. Carefully follow your plan. I already discussed the fact that your plan will be only as good as your execution of it. Follow through on every detail and stick with the investment amounts you deem appropriate to provide the cash you think you will need in retirement. If you lack the time and energy to execute your plan carefully, find someone else to do it.

3. Periodically reassess your plan. This does not mean checking your 401(k) every day and moving money from one asset to another, which could cost you a bundle in brokerage fees (if there are redemption or other transaction fees, for example) over the long haul as well as reduce your returns. It does mean looking regularly at the returns of the various assets that comprise your portfolio and evaluating whether you need to reallocate and/or rebalance them (see Chapter 6). Monitoring does not necessarily mean modifying. It simply means that you evaluate the returns of the various assets to determine whether they are still the best performers within their class. In short, do you still own the best stocks, bonds, and mutual funds for your needs?

How often is "periodically?" It depends. If you are close to retirement, you should monitor your assets more often than when you are decades away from retiring. Here are general guidelines for the frequency of assessing and, if necessary, reallocating and/or rebalancing your 401(k):

- **Semi-annually to annually, more than 12 years from retirement.** During this period, your portfolio will mostly – if not exclusively – consist of growth stocks. Though there may be rare occasions to change the allocation, the real reason for monitoring is to make sure you have the best growth stocks available.

- **Quarterly to semi-annually, between five and 12 years from retirement.** Rather than being concerned about cash flow, you will want each of your asset classes to be producing the best return for its level of risk.

- **Quarterly, within five years of retirement.** During this period, you will be making finer adjustments to your portfolio to ensure its ability to provide you the regular cash flow you require once you retire.

When I conduct public lectures and make media appearances, I tell my audiences they have only two choices to make regarding investing for retirement: 1) *Invest aggressively* and be ready for market volatility, both positive and negative, or 2) *Save aggressively* and settle in for significant growth over the long haul. As you can see, "aggressively" is the key term in both instances. A successful 401(k) strategy requires your active participation.

Do not be an ostrich. Instead, keep your head out of the sand so you can keep a close eye on your investments.

Ignorance is *Not* Bliss

Bob advises young people to "save every nickel you can because the bubble's going to burst." He chastises himself for the way he handled his own 401(k) plan. "I was ignorant about it," he says. "I should have stayed more on top of it. I might not have lost that much money."

He had an opportunity to buy AT&T stock when he began working there in 1985. At the time, the stock traded around $60 a share. The stock was "going great guns" at the time, he recalls. At one point, after AT&T divested Lucent in 1996, Lucent rose to as high as $120. AT&T was matching 50 percent of the amount that employees invested in its stock. The company was also giving employees a certain amount of stock for every $10,000 of their annual salary. Lucent continued this practice. Eventually (and following AT&T's spinning off Lucent), Bob wound up with about $125,000 worth of Lucent stock. This comprised the entirety of his 401(k) plan.

Lucent did not require employees to contribute their own money to their 401(k) plans. However, employees could volunteer to contribute the Lucent stock they bought through the company's stock-purchase plan. Bob contributed the maximum amount allowed under the 401(k) plan. Lucent prohibited its employees from moving the company's matching contributions to non-Lucent plans, at least until they resigned, retired, or were fired. However, even if Bob had been able to invest his retirement funds elsewhere, he lacked the knowledge.

When he retired officially in 2000, Lucent stock was, as he puts it, "a piece of crap." The stock was trading about $80 a share – down one-third from its high-rolling days. As he left Lucent, he collected two years' worth of salary, a full pension and full benefits, including what he calls "fairly decent" insurance coverage for medical and dental care and prescription drugs. He also received the offer of a job at Lucent's Avaya unit for two years on a need-to-work basis.

However, what most of us might regard as a generous severance package, did not come close to covering the losses Bob had suffered in his 401(k) plan. To make matters worse, the days after he retired, Lucent, then trading around $30, spun off Avaya. "If I knew in 2000 what I know now, I would have cashed in my Lucent stock," Bob says. "The guys who did cash it in then couldn't wait to get away from Lucent. They saw the handwriting on the wall." He was not alone in holding his Lucent stock when he retired. He knows many colleagues who did likewise and lost around $300,000 each. They were, he says, "ready to kill themselves because that was their life's savings."

By late 2006, Lucent was trading north of $2 and Bob's shares were worth only $11,000. This represented a nosedive of 95 percent from the $225,000 in his 401(k) plan when he retired officially in 2000."You figure that when you retire from a company after 37 years, you can kick back and work when you want to – if you have to at all," he says. "But that's not the case and nobody's hiring old guys like me. "It's not that I'm lazy or anything," he adds. "It's just that they can get young kids to do it for eight bucks an hour, where I'm used to getting $20 to $30 an hour to do telephone work."

Bob takes consolation in knowing he was not alone among his former Lucent co-workers. "I guess because of 9/11, everything went down the tubes," he says. "It's a shame that people lost all of that kind of money." He remembers telling all his friends back in 1999 to buy Lucent because it was a hot stock. "Thank God I moved out of state," he says, "because they're all mad at me now."

I am constantly amazed at employees who presume that their companies won't be the ones to get into trouble, that their company stock will retain its value. In truth, there are a lot more Enrons than Microsofts.

Think about it: If I called you and said "You should put all your retirement money in John Deere stock," you'd think I was crazy. But if you work for John Deere, it suddenly becomes okay to put all your eggs in that one basket, even though the basket may be full of holes.

Learn From His Mistakes

While Bob's friends are mad at him, Neil is upset with himself over his level of participation in his 401(k). He views his plan as his "primary source of income" when he retires, with his pension plan and Social Security benefits being his secondary source. His "stretch goal," he says, is for his investments to double to more than $800,000 when he retires, which he hopes to do in three years when he turns 60. In retirement, and with inflation factored in, he wants to live the lifestyle he has now. "Now, I may not make it – and probably won't," he adds, "but that's where I'm looking."

In 1977, Neil was a student in training at General Motors. His supervisor at the time gave him some fatherly-like advice: Contribute 100 percent of the maximum allowable amount to the company's retirement plan. The now-deceased supervisor lived "very happy and very richly," he says, and his widow is "very well off." He followed his then-supervisor's advice – without similar success. He put – and kept – his retirement money in the funds in which GM chose to invest. He was, to say the least, a passive player in his own plan. "Back in those days, I really didn't pay a lot of attention to it," he says.

He recalls receiving annual statements from GM regarding the status of his retirement plan. He filed the statements, figuring GM knew what it was doing. That is, until 1994, when he finally woke up and began to pay much more attention to his retirement plan. He regrets not having an independent investment manager well prior to hiring Scarborough Capital Management in 1994. These days, he tells anyone who will listen, "Contribute as much as you can – period" to your 401(k) plan.

Still reeling from the financial effects of his divorce, he is currently able to contribute only 6 percent of his salary to his 401(k) plan, which constitutes three-quarters of all his investments. But in the past, he had contributed almost 20 percent to the 401(k) plan – 20 percent being the maximum amount allowed at the time.

As a result, he advises young people to commit seriously to investing a certain amount of their paycheck in a retirement plan. You may have to start off small at first, which I did," he says. "Every pay raise you get, put a certain percentage of that away. Once you get into that habit, it becomes pretty easy, actually," he adds. "Most people learn to live within their means." He also urges young people to do a better job than he did of planning their lives – including their eventual retirement. In his case, loyalty prompted him to invest too heavily in his employer's stock, which he feels was short-sighted, given the fact that GM stock is now worth a small fraction of the its value at the time he invested.

Once again, it is never a good idea to build your retirement plan around one company—even if that company is your employer.

Handing Over the Keys to His Kingdom

Dick, our third ostrich, calls himself "a sixth grader" when it comes to financial-investment shrewdness. He tried to manage his own retirement plan in the early '70s without knowing how to do it well. "You listen to people in the office – the people you think know what they're talking about – and you go ahead and do what they did," he says. "I didn't even know about the funds that I was putting my money into."

He had no idea whether he was making or losing money. "Did I worry about it? No!" he says. "I don't think I was intelligent enough to know that I should be planning for my retirement. Shame on me!" This lack of worry stemmed partly from his having felt secure about getting a GM paycheck every two weeks. "If I had an employer who was shaky," he says, "maybe I would have thought about investing some other way, or making my money work better for me." Luckily, Dick has made some responsible financial decisions. For example, he and his wife put their two children through college without borrowing a penny. His wife also invested in the 401(k) plan where she worked until retiring in 2003.

Dick's 401(k) finally became an issue for him when he heard co-workers mention how well they were doing with their own plans. He went home and told his wife, "I'm tired of being the guy who listens to someone else tell me what to do with my money." His wife suggested he hire a financial planner. He kept putting it off, though, until 2000. One day, he overheard a friend say his own investments were being managed well by us. A short time later, he hired us. He praises the services and results he has received. Still, he admits he is uneasy about letting someone else manage his money. "The hardest thing for me was giving them the keys to my kingdom – even though my kingdom's small," he says. Having said this, he is glad to have a pro in his corner. "I couldn't be happier," he says. "I'm getting 8 to 9 percent growth a year!"

We rarely get to see our clients face to face. None of us has ever met Dick, which does not bother him. As a Christian, he says, he believes in Jesus "and I never met the man."

In late 2006, Dick retired at age 60 after nearly 40 years at General Motors. These days, he uses his lucrative GM pension to maintain the lifestyle his wife and he had when they were working. He draws on his 401(k) only to pay for unexpected, necessary costs. Their home mortgage is paid off, their children are off on their own, and they can buy a new car whenever they need to. He had wanted to work until he was 62. "But the 'General' made me an offer I couldn't refuse," he says. Among others things, GM gave him 15 months worth of severance pay to retire early. While many people hate the jobs they do, he is not one of them, "I loved my job," he says. "I would have worked two more years *on my head*!"

Dick will lose his regular GM salary by early 2008. He is not worried, though. "I can handle that because my wife makes a penny bleed!" he says. "Honest to God, she's the greatest person in the world for that." In fact, in retirement, he is making more money than some people who work eight hours a day, five days a week. Yet he and his wife do not spend much of it. "We like to go to Vegas and Disney World every once in a while, but my whole life is my family," he says. "I don't need a lot of money to be happy that way."

By spending conservatively in your retirement—and continuing to save—you can ensure that you'll be able to maintain a comfortable lifestyle.

Diversify, Diversify, Diversify

Lou, on the other hand, has participated actively in his 401(k) plan – and in a conservative, responsible way. He has not tried to shoot for the moon overnight. Instead, he has slowly, steadily packed his money away for the long haul. American culture teaches us not to talk about money – even with our families. As a result, he had to learn on his own how to invest well. When Lou was growing up as one of nine children, his father ran his own sawmill. The family barely scraped by. "It was pretty much hand-to-mouth for us," he says. "There was very little financial planning."

Neither did Lou's own formal education prepare him for personal investing. While in college, he took courses in micro- and macroeconomics. "But I don't ever remember a basic course in managing your money," he says. Nevertheless, he has done exceedingly well with his 401(k) plan. He attributes this success to his upbringing. "I had to do a lot of physical work, which I actually enjoyed," he says. "But I also knew I didn't want to spend my life working in the sawmill. I wanted to do something that had more leverage and gave me some security financially," he adds. "I saw how tough it was when a note was due for one of my dad's trucks, and he was trying to figure out how to cover it." In short, a conservative upbringing, a good work ethic and common sense can provide a sound education for managing your own money.

Lou doubts today's young people are doing a better job of saving and investing money than their parents did when they were young. He is correct. A 2006 study by the American Institute of Certified Public Accountants found that Americans aged 25 to 34 saved less and borrowed more in 2004 than their counterparts in 1985. In 2004, 55 percent of this age group had savings accounts, down from 65 percent in 1985. In addition, this group's average unsecured debt, including credit card debt, increased to $4,733 in 2004 – up 52 percent from $3,118 in 1985.

Younger Americans may not be alone in this regard. The 2006 Federal Reserve Survey of Consumer Finance showed the amount of American families who reported saving some money had declined to 56.1 percent in 2004 from 59.2 percent in 2001. Furthermore, 46.2 percent of American households reported credit-card debt in 2004, up from 44.4 percent in 2001. Lou feels many young people today have some interest in learning how to invest their money properly. "But I'm not sure they really pay that much attention to it," he says. "They've got too many other things going on in their lives."

Even though he likes to work with numbers, he does not go crazy recording every detail of his spending habits. "But if you have more of a high-level view of how much you're spending and what your income is each month, I think that can be valuable," he says. "And, of course, if at all possible, pay off those credit cards every month."

He took another important step as he approached retirement. While he had determined his net worth on his own, he had us validate the amount once he became our client in 2000. "Once you do this, it's pretty easy to update it," he says. "If you update it on an annual basis, you can kind of see where you are."

Still, Lou remains somewhat apprehensive. He has a regular concern that the stock market is going to take another nosedive, as it is prone to do on occasion. In 2004, driven by this concern and relying on our advice, he invested 50 percent of his 401(k) in an annuity-like investment that is guaranteed not to decline in value. He has to pay more in fees for this investment vehicle than for a 401(k). However, he regards the annuity-like investment as a safety net in case the money remaining in his 401(k) loses value.

Motivated by his investment success, he wants to talk with his Lucent co-workers about the company's 401(k) plan. No one is willing to talk with him about it, though. Most of them also hold their paycheck amounts close to the vest – even though he knows what they make because the company has defined salary levels. Asked for the most important advice he wants to give to his co-workers, he responds, "Diversify! Do not put any money in your own company because you already have a lot riding there; it is the company you are working for. If you have a long time to go before retirement, you may want to invest more of your money in the growth area, then have a financial-planning company manage your money." He likes the fact that Americans can invest their hard-earned money in 401(k) plans on a tax-free basis. And he points to the problems facing various company pension plans as well as the Social Security system. The 401(k) plans, he says, are "one of the best things going out there."

Lou began to invest in his 401(k) plan in 1970, about one year after going to work for Michigan Bell. From practically day one, he invested 10 percent of his pay – the maximum amount allowed under the plan – and the company matched two-thirds of the first 6 percent. He has continued to invest 10 percent to this day. Back in 1970, he invested 50 percent of his retirement funds in Michigan

Bell stock, feeling it was a good practice to do so because he was an employee of the firm. He put the other half in a diversified equity portfolio, which initially did not offer many choices. Eventually, he went to work for AT&T after Bell spun off its regional Bell operating companies in 1984. This was when he stopped investing any of his money in company stock, a move he feels worked well for him.

For many years, Lou was also an ostrich, failing to play an active role in managing his retirement fund. He recalls reviewing monthly statements, seeing that the plan was doing well, and not thinking of it again until the next statement arrived. "Frankly, it was on my list to do and I did not get to it very often," he says. "I always talked to people about it, but I wasn't very hands-on with it, even though I like numbers." In recent years, though, he has gotten much more hands-on with his 401(k) plan. Even though his retirement plans have done well since 1970, he believes he should have hired a professional investment firm much earlier than 2000, when he became our client. "I'm not sure my plan would have done that much better," he says. "But I would have felt better about it."

Lou is the perfect example of the classic American investor who simply drops money into a retirement account with no plan or specific goal. This kind of investor plans to retire, THEN look at his statements to determine how he'll be able to live in retirement. The smart investor takes the opposite approach: He determines how much money he needs to live comfortably and works consistently toward that goal.

CHAPTER 2 401(K)NOWLEDGE GAINS

- Make a good, realistic plan, carefully follow it, and periodically reassess it.

- Assess and, if necessary, reallocate and/or rebalance your 401(k) with the following frequencies: semi-annually to annually, more than 12 years from retirement; quarterly to semi-annually, between five and 12 years from retirement; and quarterly, within five years of retirement.

- Invest aggressively and be ready for market volatility, both positive and negative.

- Save aggressively and settle in for significant growth over the long haul.

3

Determine Your Investor Profile

Have a retirement methodology.

Most of our clients are so clueless it is frightening. Many had no retirement plan before joining us. Some had saved much money while others had saved little. In nearly all cases, they lacked a plan for arriving at retirement in financially good shape Among other things, they had not determined their investor profiles.

In Chapter 1, I shared with you the three basic stages of retirement – one or more of which you will pass through. These will help you to determine your investor profile. Here are 10 additional considerations for creating an achievable profile of your eventual life in retirement, which I first shared with you to in *The Scarborough Plan: Maximizing the Power of Your 401(k):*

- Where will you live? In your existing home? In a smaller home? In several homes?

- What will you drive? How often will you replace your car? Will you buy new or used?

- What "luxury" items will you buy? A boat? A yacht? A recreational vehicle? A chalet in Switzerland?

- What medical and health expenses could you encounter? Chronic medications? Home health care? Nursing-home care? Hospitalization?

- Will you provide financial assistance to your parents, children or grandchildren?

- What would happen to your retirement picture if your spouse dies? What if you divorce? If you are single, what if you marry?

- Will you travel? In what style? How often? To where? For how long?

- Will you contribute to charities? Establish your own foundation?

- Will you have other debts that you need to take into account?

- Do you expect to learn more about finances and managing your money? Do you need a professional financial advisor?

Completeness and detail are the most important aspects of setting your retirement goals. In your investment planning, you must make a place for them. To do this, you need to know exactly what each one requires. Otherwise, you might find yourself hunting for bear with nothing but a slingshot. The goal is specific enough – but not the planning and preparation. The bottom line: If you want to enjoy a good retirement, know exactly what you intend to do while you are living it. Figure it out. Write it down. And do not leave anything out.

Kim, Carrie, and Carol have created achievable investor profiles. As a result, they will most likely avoid the fate of dying without any money. Kim is fiscally conservative with her 401(k) and she understands well her investor profile. Carrie expects to participate actively in her 401(k) plan and her wisdom regarding her investor profile belies her age. And Carol is well on her way to becoming a millionaire in a few years.

For Neil, a legally painful divorce and the tragedy of 9/11 helped shape his investor profile. However, he is rebounding nicely. Meanwhile, a solid marriage and a sound savings ethic helped shape the investor profile of Greg and his wife. They have done a good job saving and investing money their entire adult lives. As a result, I expect them to continue these healthy habits for a long time to come.

I like our clients to have a retirement methodology. They may not know how to invest their money – that is our job. However, they need at least to know their retirement goals. I tell clients who lack such a methodology and hail from a family with a long life span: "If you follow in your family's footsteps and live for many years in retirement, you will die with no money. This is a 100 percent certainty."

A Conservative Amount of Risk

Kim hopes to live to 100. If she achieves her goal and continues to be fiscally conservative, her retirement portfolio would see several more decades of growth.

As you learned in Chapter 1, she has a planned, disciplined approach to saving and investing for retirement. She understands well her investor profile and is quite comfortable assuming a conservative degree of investment risk for her retirement plan.

"At my age now and even many years ago, I knew that I should take some risk simply because the money was going to be there in the market much longer than if I were much older," she says. "I could also *afford* the risk."

Kim could tolerate much more risk when she was younger. "As I get older, I get more conservative," she says. "As I get close to retirement, I want to save what I have." Her goal is to retire in three years at 53 — a relatively young age. "I've got many more years in which I can stand a little bit of a risk," she says. Her grandmother is 98 — longevity is in her family genes. If Kim does retire at 53, she would quite likely live in retirement for almost a half a century — much longer than she would have been in the workplace.

Kim's description of her investor profile fits exactly with our profile of her. Even if we were not managing her retirement account, she would most likely be following a similar path in her investment life. She is fairly unusual in that she stays constantly involved in her retirement account; she wakes up every day understanding what investment strategy she is pursuing and why. I only wish every investor had a touch of Kim in his/her soul.

Quite Mature Goals For Someone So Young

To Carrie, "determine your investor profile" means to work closely with your professional financial adviser. "You're working in tandem with them to make the best decisions about your investments," she says. She proclaims to be "a big research person" who "would do a lot of research on the best way to invest my money in a 401(k). I would make sure I ask my adviser questions, to make sure I take the right steps, so I have the most profitable retirement fund."

She uses the Web – particularly Google – to research potential investments. She also talks with her parents and friends for advice and tips on good investments. The numerous investment-related conversations she has had with her grandfather through the years also have prepared her well for determining her investor profile. "Ultimately, it's my decision in the end, so I'll do what I think is best," she says. "But the majority of the time, when I hear feedback from other people whose opinion I respect about their own experience, I'll listen to it."

She also tries to save as much money as possible, although she finds it difficult to do because she is starting her post-college life. She has set up one certificate of deposit and is setting up another one. Her best friend is a bank manager and helped her with the CDs. While she was awaiting entry to her company's 401(k) plan in August 2007, she bought one certificate of deposit.

Carrie learned about the stock market from her grandfather, who was an investment broker for a large, national bank. "He taught me how to read the tickers when I was eight," she says. "I've just always been interested in investing my money in stocks at some point in my life." Having grown up during the Great Depression, her grandfather has "a wonderful retirement because he saved so well for it," she says. "He didn't necessarily give up a lot during his work life. He just knew how to save and was not extravagant. Then when he retired, he traveled all over the world. He wasn't cheap – he used his money wisely."

While her grandparents saved and invested quite well for their retirement, her parents have done less well in this regard. "I think my parents are going to be working a little bit longer than they anticipated," she says. "I don't want to have to work longer than I need to. I want to make sure I set up good retirement funding and have everything in line."

Carrie views money as something to save and spend in healthy balance. "I am doing different things to enhance my lifestyle," she says. "Because I'm on my own, I want to explore everything in my city and I want new stuff for my apartment. But at the same time, I realize I need to save for a few years down the line. So I'm trying to find a happy medium so I can do both." She thinks her generation spends generally somewhat more money than previous generations. "But I think we understand, too, the need for savings," she says. "I think we are the combination of my parents' generation and my grandparents' generation. We can find pieces from both that will work for us."

One of her key short-term goals is to save enough money to attend graduate school and visit Europe with her friends in 2008. Her long-term goals are three-fold: save enough money in a bank account to pay for her wedding someday; put enough money away to eventually buy a house; and have enough money to live comfortably in retirement. In her early 20s, she understandably regards retirement as "a long way down the road." Still, she is able to envision buying a vacation home in Florida or some warmer clime and retiring there to "relax." She also wants to have enough money in retirement to travel and see the world. And she sees herself doing some paid, freelance writing – at least, in the early years of retirement.

These are quite mature goals for someone so young. Equally mature, is her view of marriage. Too few people of Carrie's age consider financial prowess when deciding whether to marry someone. She is a shining exception. For her, a marriage deal breaker would be a potential spouse who refuses to save and invest a certain minimum amount of their annual earnings. "I'd want to make sure there was going to be some money being set aside," she says. "A turn-off would be if he were a *huge* spender on stuff we don't really need. And I would hate it if he did not really take the time to think wisely about purchases or saving habits."

She does not hesitate when asked what she would do if she won the lottery tomorrow. "I'd probably invest the majority of it and maybe take a small percentage of it and go on a trip," she says. "I'd probably donate a lot of it, too, to charity." She would also continue to work. "I don't think I could ever *not* work right now in my life," she says.

Odds are, Carrie will not win the lottery anytime soon. Therefore, it is good to see her investor profile is not that of a big gambler or a high-risk taker. In fact, she clearly understands that she needs to save and strikes a healthy balance between spending and saving in her life. Actually, I'm encouraged that so many young people are good savers. Many people in their twenties seem to understand that Social Security may not be around when they're ready to retire, so they have to be responsible for their own retirements. Many older people could learn a thing or two from their children.

Doing Well After Not Having A Clue

Carol admits she was ignorant about her investor profile until her late 30s. "I didn't have a clue as to what I was doing," she says. "I didn't have a clue what a 401(k) was." She attended college for two years, majoring in business, before going to work for Southwestern Bell at age 27. She does not think her college education taught her much about saving and investing. "I learned the most from my parents," she says. "We were very, very middle-income and my parents were very independent. I saw a lot of my relatives borrowing from my grandparents and that just killed my parents. They thought that was the worst thing in the world to do."

She recalls her parents saying, "We'll starve before we take money from any of our relatives." They set a good example for her and her siblings, and she admires them for it. "We may not have had the latest and greatest car," she says. "But what we did have, my mom and dad paid for on their own" They remain this way in retirement. They don't borrow any money from us kids in any way whatsoever. They taught us kids to be the same way. Although none of us is rich, we're all very independent. None of us borrows money from our mom or dad, and we all save for retirement, just like they did."

Carol does not expect her parents, when they die, to leave any money to their children. "I don't really want them to," she says. "I want them to spend all that money on themselves, and I think they're entitled to do that. They didn't have a 401(k) plan, but they saved money anyway. That speaks volumes about my mom and dad."

When she was 27, Carol followed her parents' money-saving example. She invested in a 401(k) plan through Southwestern Bell. She did so after an older co-worker told her, "You need to get into a 401(k) plan. This is a good deal. If you start saving at your age right now, you will be a millionaire by the time you retire."

"I wasn't quite sure how I was going to do that, but that got my attention and I believed her. I've had no regrets about it at all."

Back then, Carol invested the minimum amount that her company would match, which was 6 percent. When she could afford to invest even more, she did so. Her goal was to put 14 to 16 percent of her income in the 401(k) plan, which she eventually achieved. One of her original options with the 401(k) plan was a certain guaranteed-interest fund, in which she put her money. "I went the safest way I could for many years," she says. Eventually, her company recommended professional investment advisors to its employees. She says she grew "a little older and a little wiser" after hiring one.

Before then, she had based her investment decisions on recommendations by some friends. "I just listened to people who I figured were just smart people and whom I admired," she says. "They were open enough to share their portfolio stories with me, and how well they were doing. I felt I could trust what they were saying." She says the proverbial water-cooler advice was "not so good, to tell you the truth." One older co-worker, who had convinced her to start a 401(k) plan, also urged her to invest some of her money in a Merrill Lynch mutual fund. "I respected her opinion and went with that," Carol says. "That money never went anywhere – it never did anything for me. I'm sure Merrill Lynch – although they didn't get rich off me – made money."

This episode finally opened her eyes. "I'm in the telecommunications business and that's what I'm an expert at," she says. "I figured, maybe I should be checking with somebody who's an expert at investing." In the early 1990s, she hired Scarborough Capital Management to manage her 401(k) plan. These days, Carol wishes that Roth IRAs had been available to her when she was younger. "I think those are *incredible* for younger people," she says. "Of course, I'm no expert, but you're putting away money that's going to grow at a tax-free rate. Oh my God, I wish I had gotten into that when I was 25."

She also feels companies need to provide financial education to their employees. On this, she thinks much of the business community leaves its workers high and dry. Of course, many companies may fear litigation that could result should they mishandle their employees' retirement investments. However, she views this as a lame excuse. "I think that's very unfair because in this day and age, companies expect *so much* time and effort from their employees," she says." I think they're doing their employees a *great* disservice."

She advises her younger co-workers to invest in 401(k)s. "You've got to get in on this," she tells them. "This is *free* money." Some coworkers say they cannot afford to invest in a 401(k) plan right now. Her response to them: "You can't afford *not* to get in on it."

Carol is not yet a millionaire – she has more than $450,000 in her retirement account plus some other money she and her husband have in other investments. However, she feels confident her 401(k) plan will more than double in value by the time she retires in 10 to 15 years. "I think I have a real, good shot of having well over $1 million by the time that happens," she says. She continues to be watchful of her 401(k) plan. "I do think about it at least once a week," she says. "I wonder whether it's growing at the rate I want it to grow at."

With this sort of vigilance and a good knowledge of her investor profile, Carol will likely join the Millionaire's Club in the next decade or so. Once again, it pays to stay involved in your retirement plan; benefits definitely show up on the bottom line.

Getting Burned

When Neil got married in 1987 at age 36, he had $55,000 in his 401(k) plan. By 2000, when he got divorced, the plan and his other investments had grown substantially. These days, they are worth more than $400,000. He made a big mistake by getting married without a prenuptial agreement, which could have covered his retirement and pension plans. Such plans can be subject to divorce settlements, depending on the state you live in and when you got married. "I was really stupid," he says. "But I can now pass that information on to other people." He thinks all married couples should have prenuptial agreements.

The legal system took about one year to decide how exactly Neil and his then-wife, who lacked her own retirement or pension plan, should split up their shared holdings. Their state requires a 50-50 split in terms of dollar value. The $55,000 in Neil's 401(k) plan when he got married was not subject to the split, which occurred only three days after the tragic events of September 11, 2001. Because the $55,000 amount was fixed in time, it did not depreciate when the stock market plunged in the wake of the terrorist attacks of 9/11. However, the remainder of his and his then-wife's investment portfolio did fall significantly in value post 9/11. And his ex-wife did receive what he calls "a six-figure number" when they split their holdings.

A prenuptial agreement could have prevented this. "I just couldn't believe the figure she was going to get for being married to me" for less than 12 years, Neil says. "It was just astronomical. "I'm still scrambling to this day to make up that deficit. Having to buy the house *twice,* has put me even further behind. But I still have my head above water."

One financial life preserver is the large pay raise he got in 2006. As a result, he plans to resume the maximum contribution to his 401(k) plan sometime in 2007. He has at least one other good thing going for him: He has a good idea of how to invest properly so he can eventually retire in comfort. And he is doing a great job of saving money for retirement. Thanks to his recent pay raise, he will soon be contributing even more to his 401(k) plan.

With a bit of luck and decent financial markets, and if Neil sticks to his investor profile, he should be able to retire when he turns 60. He should also be able to live comfortably in retirement.

Good Savers All Their Lives

Greg says he and his wife, Cathy, were raised to "save, save, save." This is their investor story and they are sticking to it. Greg had what he calls a "tough" upbringing. His father ran his own business, which did not do well at times, impacting the family's standard of living. As a reaction to this periodic deprivation as a child, he says he spent "a little more than I should have" when he left the Navy. However, he quickly brought those spending habits under control, avoiding a credit-card debt problem. He received good financial counseling while in the Navy Reserves and from one of his fellow reservists, who worked for a local bank.

The most debt Greg has ever racked up was $1,200, which is a rounding error for many people in debt. And Cathy, he says, is even more debt-adverse than he is. "As much as we wanted material things, we understood that we could get into trouble with too much debt," he says. "There are things we can find to enjoy without being extravagant and stupid with the money."

Greg began working for General Motors 30 years ago, right out of the Naval Reserve. Initially, he and Cathy attempted to manage his GM investment plan on their own. Throughout his employment, they have invested the maximum allowable amount in the plan. One day, he talked with some fellow employees and realized he and his wife were letting a good opportunity slip by them. "I didn't have a clue as to what I was doing," he says. At that time, GM sent its employees a quarterly statement reporting where their funds were invested and how those investments were performing. His plan kept doing well. As a result, he and Cathy failed to pay much, if any, attention to the plan until the arrival of the next quarterly statement, which usually showed continual gains. He recalls thinking, "Wow, this looks pretty cool. Maybe we should pay more attention to it."

Finally, in 1994, Greg teamed up with us; at the time, we had been managing investments for many other GM employees. He and Cathy decided they lacked the skills to continue managing his portfolio on their own. Furthermore, his job as district field manager required him to drive several hours a day. This gave him little or no time to keep up with his investments or to discuss them with Cathy. These days, he thinks he waited too long to hire a professional financial adviser. "I wish I had done that when I first started with GM," he says. Back then, GM informed its employees that firms such as ours are available to assist them with their retirement investments. The employees decided which, if any, firm to hire.

He has advised his three sons and one daughter to begin setting aside money for their retirement as soon as possible, and to invest as much as possible. Referring to the "big-time trouble" one of his sons got into in recent years with credit-card debt, he says young people need to avoid too much debt. "The only things you should owe money on, are a house and a car – and only *one* car," he says. He reports the son in question is now "getting himself straightened out." He says he perceives another spending "just flat too much, but I've got to sit there and keep my mouth shut other than to say, 'Save, save, save.'"

Referring to his own mortality, Greg has told his sons and daughter, "I hope you've got enough money to bury me when I die." He thinks his youngest son and daughter understand and take him seriously. "Of course, my wife and I feel that we'd like to leave something for them," he says. "But if there's nothing there, they'd better be ready to handle life on their own."

Greg says he and Cathy, who also remains employed and has her own 401(k) plan, are "pretty practical." Therefore, despite his half-in-jest warnings to his children, he does not see them spending all of their retirement money before they die. "We're going to want to travel, but we don't need to travel on the QE II," he says. "Also, I'd like to buy a nicer car, be it a Cadillac, an Impala, or an Avalanche. Then, we're off to see the country. Some nights, we'll get a cheap motel. Some nights, we'll spend some more and get a fancy place. We'll eat sandwiches for three days and then go out and have a grand dinner somewhere."

Based on their fine history of saving and investing for retirement, I expect Greg and Cathy to enjoy their fair share of driving, hostelling, and dining luxuriously in retirement.

CHAPTER 3 401(K)NOWLEDGE GAINS

- Define completely and in detail the investment risk that you can assume plus the retirement lifestyle that you seek.
- Calculate exactly how much you will need in your retirement account.
- Determine how long it will be before you must tap into your retirement savings.
- Hire and work closely with a professional financial adviser.
- Obtain a prenuptial agreement with your spouse-to-be, or a post-nuptial agreement with your spouse.

4

Allocate Your Plan's Assets Appropriately

Avoid outright gambling.

You should feel free to put all your 401(k) money in the stock market only as long as you invest in companies with which you are familiar and comfortable. Think twice, though, before investing all of your retirement funds in a single industry or stock. This amounts to outright gambling.

Gary crossed this line during the "dot.bomb" era. He invested too much of his money in Internet stocks. The loss he suffered did not financially break him, but to this day, it hurts when he thinks about it. Each of us has our "play money;" we play with it when we believe an investment is truly hot. However, when we play with our retirement money, we are idiots! And we will most likely get burned.

There are four sets of equity criteria that you need to consider when allocating your plan's assets appropriately:

1. **Market size.** small, mid, and large.
2. **Investment style.** growth, value, and blend.
3. **Geographic scope.** Domestic, international, and global.
4. **Management.** Active or passive.

You also need to realize that your retirement portfolio today will not be the same as five or 12 years from now. Typically, there are three different types of retirement portfolios. The one you need to be in right now depends on how close to – or far from – retirement you are.

The following descriptions of portfolio types, taken from my book, *The Scarborough Plan: Maximizing the Power of Your 401(k)*, will be helpful in analyzing our subjects' investment styles.

1. **Portfolio A.** If you are more than 12 years away from needing cash flow from your retirement plan, have an aggressive allocation of assets. The investments should be heavily tilted toward growth stocks, including stocks of smaller companies. All the

historical data support a diversified portfolio substantially, if not exclusively, invested in growth stocks.

2. **Portfolio B.** If you are between five and 12 years from needing the cash flow, your portfolio should include a substantial number of growth stocks or growth-stock funds as well as some of the income-producing elements that will comprise your investment portfolio at the end of this period. As you get closer to retirement, the allocation of assets should be gradually changed from a more aggressive mix (emphasizing growth stocks) to a more conservative mix (emphasizing value stocks, dividend-paying stocks and bonds.)

3. **Portfolio C.** If you are within five years of needing the cash flow, the allocation of your portfolio of assets should be fairly conservative. At this stage and throughout your retirement, you want to be assured of an income stream with a minimal risk of losing the value of your principal. For this reason, your portfolio should include such as stocks or funds with a consistent history of paying dividends, high-grade corporate bonds or funds, and U.S. Treasury instruments.

Keep in mind that the difference between these three portfolios is not based on your age now or when you die. It is based solely on when you need to begin generating cash flow from your retirement plan.

Because considerable knowledge and experience are required to evaluate and select from among these equity criteria and retirement portfolios, I do not advise most of you to try managing your own 401(k) plans. Andrew is an exception to this rule. Clearly, he has a good understanding of investing and a great handle on his retirement plan. The way he manages his plan does not make me nervous.

I cannot say the same thing about many of the other people I profiled in this book. Therefore, I advise most of you to hand the responsibility for appropriate asset allocation to a professional financial planner. When you do this, you must remain an active player in the allocation game. Bearing witness to this key piece of 401(k) knowledge are Stephanie, Kim, Wendy, Omar, Ann, and Jennifer.

Play Keno and Have A Couple Drinks

In the early '90s, Gary hired Scarborough Capital Management to manage his investment funds. He also bought and sold stocks on his own through a broker. He began playing the market by investing $2,500 in some stocks upon advice from family and friends. Appropriate allocation of his plan's assets was the furthest thing from his mind.

"I just kind of dabbled in stocks and some of them worked out okay," he says. "But when I look back at *all* the stocks I bought, I probably lost my butt on them." He figures he finished "about 10 grand in the hole." Because of this bad experience, he adopted and tried to follow a firm rule for himself: Never take stock advice from friends and relatives. Looking at his history, it is clear why he formulated that rule.

Initially, he made some money investing in a startup for which his brother-in-law was an executive. After the company founders sold the firm and started yet another business, He invested $10,000 in their latest venture: a dot.com operation. "I lost my butt on that one, big time, during the 'dot.bomb' era," he says. "It hurts to think about it. I don't really buy stocks now on my own."

Gary wants to retire when he is 62 – nine years from now – and begin drawing cash from his 401(k). This puts him squarely in Portfolio B. His vision of retirement would have him working only three days a week. "And not as the greeter at Wal-Mart, either," he chuckles. He also sees himself playing golf at least a couple days a week. In addition, his home mortgage will finally be paid off as long as he continues making the same monthly payments he now makes. Once the house is paid off, he will tap into the home equity to buy a new pick-up truck.

These days, Gary is in great financial shape – and not only because he has taken our advice. He maintains a healthy savings and prudent spending ethic. He also successfully resists the urge to play the stock market. Instead, he says, "I go to the bar, play Keno, and have a couple of drinks. Actually, I'm a little bit ahead, playing about 40 bucks a week."

Clearly, Gary understands the difference between gambling and investing for your retirement. A little responsible, recreational gambling can be fun, but gambling with your retirement account is tantamount to playing Russian Roulette.

Today's Variable Annuities Are Fabulous

While Barbara is not a client of ours, she also seems to be in good shape for retirement, which she hopes will happen in the next year or two. Still, she has some concerns about some of her investments. For the last 15 years, she has had her retirement money in a 401(k) plan plus two variable annuities and is less than fully satisfied. "I'm not really happy with the performance of one of the variable annuities," she says. "I have in the back of my mind to move that money elsewhere, but I haven't done it yet."

Barbara's concern about variable annuities is understandable. Yes, they are the most expensive method you can use to manage your money. The cost of the required account insurance is around 0.5 percent. However, today's variable annuities can produce excellent investment returns for you.

I have been in the financial-investment business for 25 years. During the first 21, I never touched a variable annuity for a client. The major reason: They were designed for the people who sold them and for the corporations to which they sold them. However, they were *not* designed for the employees of those corporations.

A variable annuity guarantees the principal amount that you invest, yet you invest your money exactly as you would with a 401(k).

Therefore, you avoid all the risk and realize all the reward. You also get to invest your retirement money in best-of-class assets. Furthermore, today's variable annuities guarantee a 5 to 6 percent annual return. In a worst-case scenario, every $100 you invest at the beginning of a year will be worth at least $105 to $106 at the end of that year.

In recent years, the variable-annuity portfolios that we have managed for The Hartford and Pacific Life have outperformed the 401(k) plans we have managed for Lucent Technologies, AT&T, and General Electric, among many other clients. Today's variable annuities are fabulous. Tell me another way I can eliminate all risk and still make money for you! I am certainly unaware of any.

Having said this, we refuse to put all of our client's retirement money in variable annuities. This is simply because we do not want them to have to pay insurance on *all* their investments. For more than 70 percent of our working and retired clients, we invest at least 50 percent of their retirement money in variable annuities. Typically, we invest a client's money in insured variable annuities and the rest in uninsured investments. Even if the uninsured investments decline in value, at least half of the client's portfolio would be protected.

One more caveat: While it is okay to buy a variable annuity, never *annuitize* money. "Annuitizing" means you pay, say, $100 to the insurance company. In return, the insurer pays you 5 to 6 percent interest until you die. And when you die, the insurance company does not pay any money to your estate. In short, you will have given your original $100 payment to the insurer.

Some people say, "Annuities stink!" Well, they stink when you annuitize!

Variable annuities are not necessarily for everybody. Some of our clients have so much money that they do not need to insure it. Even if the value of their retirement account declined by half, they would still be fine. The only time they need to insure their money is when they plan to leave it to their children or a charity when they die.

On the flip side of this same coin, if you have only, say, $200,000 in your retirement account, you should insure *every dime* of it. You cannot afford a large drop in the market.

Returning to Barbara's story, she relies on her company's investment-plan manager to direct her retirement investments. Her behavior underscores yet another great misperception many people have. They believe incorrectly that either an internal manager of their own company, and/or an external investment firm such as Fidelity or T. Rowe Price is responsible for making investment decisions for them.

In fact, such parties are only record keepers. Even when they actually manage a company's retirement fund, they do so only for the company – not for its employees. This practice is quite common in the American business world. It is also quite wrong when it comes to the financial needs of employees such as Barbara.

Not Too Difficult For Novices

Andrew does not share this misperception at all. Thanks to his educational background and professional experience, he has done a fine job of allocating his assets appropriately during the three and one-half years he has had a 401(k) plan. He pays active attention to the markets through either day trading or managing his plan and tends to focus on emerging markets globally. Half of his plan is in international funds and he recently switched the other half from small-cap to large-cap stocks.

Unlike most people with 401(k) plans, Andrew is steeped in the ways of saving and investing. He has an undergraduate degree in business administration, is seeking an MBA, and worked for National City Bank immediately prior to Cardinal Health. "I have learned a lot of this on my own," he says. "I do spend a lot of time researching markets and stocks. I do watch the evening TV shows such as Jim Cramer's *Mad Money* on CNBC. If I could project where I want to be in five years, it would be running my own capital-management firm."

He does not think a 401(k) plan is too difficult for financial novices to handle. "A friend of mine has a background in instructional design, not finance," he says. "She has all these fears because she doesn't have a financial background and doesn't understand it. She has taken some finance classes and is starting to learn a little bit of it."

Most people are not as deeply involved with finance and investment as Andrew is. However, I agree with him that you do not need to be an expert to be an active participant in your 401(k) plan. Indeed, you must play an active role in all aspects of your retirement portfolio, including appropriate allocation of its assets.

Time To Revisit the Plan

Where Andrew plays this sort of an active role, Wendy does not. Based on a recent workplace experience, she is now rethinking her approach to her retirement plan.

Federal Realty Investment Trust hires Prudential to manage its 401(k) plan. In 2003, Prudential asked Wendy and her fellow employees to complete an investor-profile workbook. Among other things, they were asked about the value of their assets and when they plan to retire. Wendy displayed a "moderate risk" profile and relied on Prudential to allocate appropriately her plan's assets based on her profile. Whenever she has questions about or needs to make changes in her plan, she can either call a Prudential agent or visit the Prudential website.

Generally speaking, the process Prudential uses is a good one. However, there are two fatal flaws. One, Prudential does not consider all of the assets belonging to a plan holder's family. This is because these assets are quite difficult to quantify. Two, Prudential fails to recognize that *when* you plan to retire has absolutely nothing to do with how you manage your retirement money. *When you are going to need the money* is the real issue. It could be before you retire, or it could be after.

Wendy and her husband, Ben, are expecting their first child. Conceivably, she could leave the workplace for several years to raise children. And she could either not return to work or quit working altogether once she is 50. Along the way, Wendy and Ben could come into a large amount of money perhaps because of a big inheritance. As a result, Wendy may not need to touch her retirement money until she is 70.

When you eventually retire has nothing to do with appropriately allocating your assets. Appropriate allocation has everything to do with planning for *when you eventually need to tap the money in your retirement account.* This is news to Wendy. "I have not revisited my plan since 2003, when I signed up for it, and I probably should revisit it," she says. "After this interview, I am going to contact Prudential and change some of my allocations."

Wendy is not alone in this regard. The way Prudential manages her 401(k) plan is the norm for how we manage money in America. As we invest initially in our 401(k) plan, we make certain allocation decisions. Most of us then fail to revisit our plan to determine whether we should reallocate our money. We make this mistake even though we may have experienced all sorts of life-changing events in the interim. In Wendy's case, she has gotten married and become pregnant since the first and only time she reviewed her retirement plan.

Wendy has yet to revisit her allocations because "I didn't know the right questions to ask." However, she does know she is putting her money away for retirement in 25 to 30 years – not for a short-term goal such as buying a house. I recommend that you revisit and, if necessary, reallocate your retirement portfolio every two to three years. You should do so sooner if you go through a life-altering event such as childbirth.

A new child is a long-term liability, and you need the money to support this liability until the child is essentially "off the books." That is, until the child graduates from college and enters the full-time workplace. As long as this or any other major liability remains your responsibility, you need to regularly review your retirement plan. And when you do, you need to *reallocate* and *rebalance* your assets appropriately. (See Chapter 6.)

Mindful Acquiescence

Stephanie also needs to become a more active participant when it comes to allocating her plan's assets appropriately. When she hired us six years ago to manage her 401(k) plan, she was heavily invested in General Motors. Then, as now, GM stock was not doing well. She regards the $365 annual fee she pays us as an incentive to do business with us. "If I can pay someone to help me earn $1 a day or more, and it costs me only $1 a day, then I should do it," she says.

She would like to be more involved with her retirement plan. "But at this point in my life I really don't have any interest in being more involved," she says. "Some people may think I'm *crazy*!" She realizes she is not comfortable managing her own money. She also is comfortable acquiescing – *mindfully* as opposed to mindlessly – that responsibility to a professional manager. However, she does work closely with us when we allocate and reallocate her investments. She understands and is comfortable with this responsibility.

Stephanie shares annually what she calls her "fluctuation-tolerance levels" with her Scarborough Capital Management advisor. "They've stayed within my boundaries," she says. "The funds that I'm invested in have grown, with the exception of technology, where everything went down. The growth has pretty much been consistent – no large fluctuations."

This helps Stephanie sleep better at night. So, too, does "knowing that the money is there and growing for retirement. I try to mark that little worry off my list each night," she says. "I *feel* the money is going to be there when I'm ready to use it."

Short of winning Powerball, Stephanie, 40, is many years from retirement. As a result, she needs to have a Portfolio A type of retirement plan – one that has an aggressive allocation of assets.

Like most investors, Stephanie needs to understand that there are times when her account will go up and others when – based on prevailing economic conditions – it will go down in value. Once she clearly understands that there is a natural ebb and flow to retirement investing, she'll feel more comfortable about sticking to her long-term goals, resisting the temptation to indulge in knee-jerk reactions.

Stuck In A Crappy Plan

Omar, 34, is also right for Portfolio A. While he is not our client, he seems to be managing his retirement plan well. His problem, however, is that he is stuck in the federal government's retirement system, which has only five investment options. Calling this amount of options "sub par" is a real understatement.

Despite the fact that his hands are tied behind his back, he is doing the best he can.

He has invested 75 percent of the $30,000 in his 401(k) plan in stocks and the rest is in Treasury notes. He contributes a total of about $600 a month, or about 8 percent of his salary, to the plan.

Prior to going to work for the Treasury Department, Omar was employed by a company in the private sector. He contributed about $100 a month to the company's Roth IRA plan and now has about $16,000 in this plan. His 401(k) plan through the federal government is doing much better than his Roth IRA plan through his former employer. While the 401(k) is invested in domestic and international stocks, the Roth IRA is in only domestic stocks.

Omar has invested most of his retirement funds in stocks, taking an aggressive approach because he does not plan to retire until he is in his 60s. "Stocks are so volatile," he says. "They change a lot over time, but I felt I could afford the time for my investments to even out, since my retirement is a way down the road." He made his allocation choices after doing research and talking with "people who were older than I was and people who were close to retirement." He is not a client of ours and does not consult a professional financial advisor because the Treasury Department does not make such advisors available to Omar and his coworkers.

Neither does the federal government's 401(k) plan allow employees to move their retirement funds into other plans with more options. (These are called "in-service withdrawals.") Even if the government did allow its employees to do so, the limitations on the amount of money these employees could withdraw from their plan prior to reaching age 59½, would be modest at best.

While Omar does not have the best of 401(k) plans, he will be fine with it as long as he continues to have an investment methodology and stick to it. He will run into trouble only if he chases after short-term gains, or takes a passive role with his plan. I call this behavior "driving a car by looking in a rear-view mirror." Too many people manage their retirement money this way and get into financial trouble as a result. Omar, on the other hand, drives his retirement investment with his focus fixed on the road ahead.

Perfectly Comfortable With Fluctuations

Ann also drives her 401(k) plan with her eyes peering through the windshield. However, she needs to pay more attention to an important roadside sign – the one reminding her to pay regular attention to the allocation of her retirement portfolio. "I do feel I should be spending more time keeping up with it and checking in on it," she says. "I did a fair amount of research upfront when I first allocated it, and then I kind of forgot about it."

Nevertheless, she at least has a good understanding of the meaning of the phrase "appropriate allocation." To her, it is relative, depending on the specific needs and desires of each investor. "Appropriate for me would be different than for someone of a different age or with different goals," she says.

Ann advises other people "to be much safer than I am being." She was aggressive with her allocations "100 percent by design," she says, and not by neglect. She also says she was "somewhat geeky at times," having created a spreadsheet to track her investments. Her spreadsheet contained the basic details and Morningstar ratings for each of the investment choices available through her 401(k) plan. She segregated the investments in the spreadsheet by type of fund – large cap, mid cap small cap, value growth, international and domestic.

While researching her eventual allocations, Ann went back 10 to 15 years on each potential investment and compared them with each other. She picked the funds that showed historically higher returns. "I figure I have a really long timeline before retirement," she says. "I'm perfectly comfortable with fluctuations." She also has a healthy attitude regarding her response to fluctuations. She expects to adhere to her methodology when the market goes up and not abandon it when the market tanks.

Ann has an undergraduate degree in psychology. She learned how to manage her own personal finances only about two years ago. "My mind doesn't go that way naturally," she says. "I was always strong in the humanities and that sort of thing. It really wasn't until I got out of law school and faced the reality of a huge amount of debt that I had to deal with, that I realized I really had to get a grip on managing personal finances," she adds. "That's when I started reading about it, watching [personal-finance expert] Suze Orman on TV and learning what this is all about."

Because Ann is not a client of ours, I am not familiar with her 401(k) plan and cannot say whether she has allocated her money appropriately. However, I can say she has a good idea of what to do and how to do it. I advise her to apply her methodology on a more regular basis. If she does so between now and when she retires eventually in two or three decades, she should be in good financial shape.

A Good Game Plan

Jennifer, who works in the same law firm as Ann, also understands well the concept of appropriate allocation. Jennifer, however, plays a much more active role in her plan. She makes a good-faith effort each month to invest the maximum allowable amount in the firm's 401(k) plan. She makes the same effort to consult monthly with her financial advisor at A.G. Edwards, with whom she has done business for 10 years.

"I ask her what the best course of action is," Jennifer says. "Do I need growth or stability? Do I need to take a bigger risk than I have been taking?" Some people do not hire professional financial planners until they are in their 20s or 30s. Jennifer hired one when she was only 18.

She began working part-time at another law firm when she was 16. Her boss at the time had invested in two mutual funds, and her job was to open the office mail. One day, Jennifer opened and read the latest monthly statement from her boss's financial advisor. "I started working out the growth and she was having a great return on these funds – this was impressive," she says. "When you're making $5 an hour, as I was then, it looked like a substantial amount of money."

At the time, she lived with her parents and had few bills. So she decided to invest most of her paycheck. She met with a financial planner – the same one with whom she has been for 10 years. The advisor told her she had a good head on her shoulders and helped her invest $50 a month in mutual funds – the same ones in which she is invested 10 years later. She has not made many changes in the allocation of her 401(k) plan over the past decade. Basically, her portfolio consists of a few risk funds, a few funds that track the S&P 500, industries that are booming and emerging economies that are politically stable.

While Jennifer has been saving and investing since she was 18, she is still at the beginning of her work career. As a result, she probably has a few decades to save and invest before she retires. While I am not familiar with her retirement portfolio, she seems to have good game plan and idea of how to execute it. She also relies heavily on advice from her financial planner. I expect Jennifer to maintain her winning ways. Presuming she does so, I anticipate she will enjoy a comfortable life during her working and retirement years.

CHAPTER 4 401(K)NOWLEDGE GAINS

- You should feel free to put all your 401(k) money in the stock market only as long as you invest in companies with which you are familiar and comfortable Think twice before investing all of your retirement funds in a single industry or stock.

- Do not play with your retirement money. You will most likely get burned!

- Consider four sets of equity criteria when allocating your plan's assets: market size, investment style, geographic scope, and management style.

- Choose the correct retirement portfolio based on when you will need the cash flow: Portfolio A (an aggressive allocation of assets), if you are more than 12 years away from needing cash flow from your retirement plan; Portfolio B (a substantial number of growth stocks or growth-stock funds plus some income-producing elements); if you are between five and 12 years from needing the cash flow or Portfolio C (a fairly conservative allocation), if you are within five years of needing the cash flow.

- Everything you might have heard about variable annuities in the past was true: They were *lousy*. This is no longer the case, though.

- I do *not* advise most people to manage their 401(k) plans on their own. However, if you have a good understanding of and ability for appropriate allocation of your plan's assets, you might want to give it a try.

- I *do* advise most people to hand responsibility for appropriate asset allocation to a professional financial planner. However, you must remain an active player in the allocation game.

5

Limit Your Plan's Exposure to Company Stock

It *can* happen to you.

Most of us think bad things happen to other people, not to us. Think back to when Lucent or Enron stocks crashed and burned. You might have thought, "This could never happen to my company. I know it too well." If you had worked for Lucent back in 1999, you might never have thought its stock price would plummet nearly 100 percent. Yet this is exactly what happened.

We cannot "read our company" to see whether it is going to falter. We also cannot know whether our company is either poorly managing or stealing from its 401(k) plan until the damage is already done. The money in our 401(k) plans is ours—and we are responsible for it. We face certain risks by putting our money in such a retirement plan. Some risks, such as an overall drop in the stock market, we cannot avoid. Other risks we can avoid, such as putting too much of our retirement money in our company's stock.

I have two thoughts about company stock, which I first shared in *The Scarborough Plan: Maximizing the Power of Your 401(k)*. One, you should ordinarily limit your company's stock to no more than 10 percent of your portfolio. The main reason has to do with diversification of your life's assets. As an employee, you are already depending upon the success of the company to provide you a regular income while you work there.

Depending on the company's success to provide you a substantial retirement nest egg, is another form of putting all those eggs in one basket. It is just too risky. Two, if your company matches your 401(k) contribution in company stock, find out whether you can transfer out of company stock and into some other asset(s). Surely, a company match is good, but it would be much better if you could allocate the match yourself. Whether or not your boss believes it, there might be a better investment for *you* than your company's stock.

Unfortunately, most 401(k) plans include substantially fewer invest-ment choices than these asset classes: growth-stock mutual funds (large-, mid-, and small-cap stocks); value-stock mutual funds (large-, mid-, and small-cap stocks); international-stock mutual funds; international-bond mutual funds; corporate-bond mutual funds; government-bond mutual funds; guaranteed-investment contracts; and market-index funds. However, the trend in Corporate America is to provide employees with additional choices. In many cases, your company will be receptive to requests by its employees to expand the assets available for investment – especially, if it does not mean increased costs to the company.

Most company executives participate in company 401(k) plans, so they will be interested in having the best plan the company can afford. A few well-chosen words about diversification, asset allocation, and the "efficient frontier" (where your portfolio can achieve the highest return possible for any particular level of risk) should suffice to grab their attention and gain their support for expanding the investment choices in your plan. (For more on the "efficient frontier," see *The Scarborough Plan: Maximizing the Power of Your 401(k)*, Chapter 3, "What You Need to Know About Asset Allocation.")

Ron, whom we will meet later, presumed his company would never face serious financial problems. Therefore, he invested a large amount of his retirement money in its stock. He was dead wrong. These days, he wonders whether he will be able to achieve his retirement goal. He has learned about investing at the proverbial School of Hard Knocks.

Kim has gotten her education at the School of Soft Landings. When her company's stock rebounded after a sharp decline, she did not invest more of her retirement money in it. She continues to resist the urge to do so. Carrie says she also would resist the urge to invest too heavily in her company's stock, even if the company were Disney, which she loves.

Neil and Dick, on the other hand loved their company too much. As a result, they had too much of their 401(k) money in its stock. Carol, though, has avoided this mistake and her common sense has paid off well for her.

I wish I could say most Americans have learned valuable lessons from Lucent, Enron, Color Tile and other public companies that lost most, if not all, their stock value in recent years. The truth is that most people who work for crash-and-burn companies are oblivious to the warning signs. We might regard our company's leaders and managers as a bunch of idiots. However, we also might find comfort in a false rationalization: "All is well because my company appears to be doing well."

Fortunately for us, our federal legislators have significantly loosened corporate restrictions on 401(k) plans in recent years. Federal law now prohibits our companies from requiring us to invest their 401(k) or other retirement monies in company stock.

They also no longer can require us to hold employee-purchased and/or company-matched stock until we reach the age of 59½. These sorts of corporate practices had caused many of us to become terribly overloaded in company stock. They left us with no way out.

In the wake of the Enron scandal in particular, our companies tripped over each other in a heated race to allow us to move money from company stock to other investments. They wanted desperately to avoid the bad press that had befallen Enron and its ilk. Why, then, do too many of us continue to invest too much of our 401(k) funds in our company's stock? We are clearly gambling that our company will prosper and thrive at least until we retire or die.

Fat, Dumb, and Happy

When Ron was a young man in the early 1970s, he was, to use his own words, "fat, dumb, and happy" regarding his retirement plan. These days, he is wiser and sadder. In 1973, he became a salaried manager for C&P Telephone Company in West Virginia, then a part of the AT&T-owned Bell System. At the time, Bell offered its salaried employees a long-term savings plan. The plan contained three investment options: AT&T stock; a guaranteed-interest plan; and a diversified-equity portfolio. He put most of his retirement money in AT&T stock. "I thought that was the bread-and-butter of the world at that time," he says. "I was really thinking that by the time I got to be 50, I'd be able to retire."

He worked for AT&T through 1984, when federal anti-trust regulators broke apart the Bell System. He left the company in the early 1990s to take a job elsewhere. He will miss his retirement goal by a decade. "I've sort of blown that. I'm 60 now and I'm still working," he says. "I don't understand that. I just want to quit." He figures he will need to work another year or two before he can afford to retire. In addition, once he does retire, he will continue to work part-time. He will not do it for the money, but instead to keep busy doing something productive. "I don't want to do the five-day-a-week thing," he says. "I want to do something a little more out of my field. I'd like to mow grass on a golf course two or three days a week," he adds. "That'd be okay." Even now, he is unsure whether he can meet his semi-retirement goal. "It all depends on this economy," he says.

Early in his career, Ron learned about investing the hard way. "It was mostly trial-and-error and word-of-mouth from people I thought knew more than I did," he says. "I never acquired the services of any financial planner at that time." At the time, AT&T had no in-house or outsourced investment-advice resources for Ron and his fellow employees. Both then and a decade later, when AT&T divested its Baby Bells, most large and small American businesses lacked such resources. These days, though, most large American companies as well as many of their small counterparts have 401(k) plans. They also employ managers trained to oversee these plans.

Ron now works for American Systems, a small federal-government contractor in Virginia. American Systems has a 401(k) plan as well as a trained plan manager. He does not participate in American System's plan. However, he does have a professional investment advisor and has been with us since the mid '90s. "Until that point, I was pretty much just shooting in the dark and using what I thought was decent information from people who had walked that walk," he says. "I had no real help."

In the mid '90s, he thought he was making no mistakes in managing his 401(k) plan on his own. This was before AT&T's stock price plummeted, and Ron realized he needed help. "I was a victim of ignorance by not knowing what I was doing," he says. He now draws a pension from Lucent, which, he observes, "is not in the greatest of shape." Through Lucent, he also receives health benefits, which the company has considerably pared in recent years.

Two of the eliminated benefits were family health-insurance coverage and the so-called "death benefit." The latter had required Lucent to match the last year of an employee's salary upon his or her death. Ron fears Lucent, which merged in 2006 with French company Alcatel, may also eliminate its pension program. He spends nearly 40 percent of his pension on health insurance. "That's one scary thing," he says. "I would just like to be able to feel that I was locked in on the health benefits between now and when my wife and I are 65."

In the School of Hard Knocks, Ron has learned two basic retirement-planning mistakes that most of us make: 1) we do not save and invest any money for retirement; and 2) we do save and invest retirement money, but without professional advice and assistance. He puts himself squarely in the second camp. Before hiring us, he says, "I thought I was doing fine. I really wasn't doing fine, but I just didn't know it."

Like all-too-many people, Ron learned that investing in single-stock issues is the second biggest mistake people make when investing in 401(k)s; it's second only to not investing at all.

Keeping Your Distance

Kim has avoided one of Ron's mistakes. She has not put too much of her 401(k) money in her company's stock – or any other stock. When AT&T became Lucent in the mid '90s, she was laid off for an extremely brief period – only one day. AT&T let her go on a Friday and Lucent hired her back the following Monday. This gave her practically no time to get to the unemployment office.

However, the layoff status allowed her to roll the funds in her 401(k) plan into an IRA, which she did. The IRA provided broader investment options than the 401(k) plan, which she regarded as good news because she realized she had too much of her retirement money invested in her company's stock. "Getting rid of my AT&T stock was like getting rid of Mom and apple pie," she says. "It was very hard for me to let that stock go because of the sense of pride I had in AT&T."

She allowed us to reinvest the money in her AT&T holdings in other stocks. "Their advice to diversify was a good thing," she says. "I am paying them for their advice, so I should take their advice.'" To her credit, she resisted the urge to act as too many of our clients do in a situation like this. They tell us to invest their money back into their company's stock when the price begins to rise after a significant fall. For her, this was a difficult urge to resist. For several years following AT&T's spin-off of Lucent, Lucent's stock price rose as much as 30 percent a year. Some observers thought it would never stop going up.

Of course, Lucent stock eventually obeyed the laws of market gravity and fell almost 100 percent. Some of our clients who stuck with Lucent despite our advice to get out fired us. Some of them lost literally everything. For one client, the value of his 401(k) plan fell from hundreds of thousands of dollars to less than $10,000. All because he insisted on staying the course with Lucent even as it crashed and burned.

...Not Even Disney

Carrie's current employer does not offer company stock to its employees. However, when she was in college, she worked part-time at Gap, a national clothing retailer that gave its employees the opportunity to buy company stock. She did not take advantage of the opportunity, though, because she needed all of her pay for college expenses. These days, she would still hesitate to invest in a stock like Gap. "If the company is successful, then you are going to be, too, but you run a risk when you work at a company like Gap, whose business is trends and styles. Its stock fluctuates a good deal," she says, adding, "I would be nervous to invest in a retail company. Right now, Gap is not at the top of market among retail clothing stores."

Would she invest a large portion of her retirement money in any large, public company?

"I've always wanted to work for Disney," she responds. "I think if I worked for Disney, I'd put money in that stock." A lot of it? "I don't think I could do a lot at any place," she answers. "It would be a small percentage. I don't think I'd do more than 10 percent." Like Kim, Carrie understands well the pitfalls of investing too much of retirement funds in the stock of her company – or any company, even a well-performing one like Disney.

From Naïve to Grateful

Gary has come to the same understanding. It took him a while, though, to get there. Several years ago, when he still worked for General Motors, the company's stock was doing poorly – although not as poorly as now. He thought it would be a good idea to put all of his 401(k) money in GM stock. You know: Buy low, sell high. "I was kind of naïve about stuff like that," he says. "My advisor told me *not* to do that." Gary followed his sound advice.

These days, he is grateful for doing so – especially in light of the beating Detroit is taking. "Look at Ford," he says. "In the '80s, its stock was three bucks. Then, it went up higher than $30. Then when it got back down to $16, everybody was buying it again." One of his friends had a lot of his own 401(k) money in Ford stock, which is now around $10. "He's basically got to leave his money there or take his licks and get out of it," Gary says.

Carrie, Kim and Gary have all learned the importance of maintaining a diverse portfolio. Although we've said it again in this book, it bears repeating once more: Never put all your eggs in one basket, even if that basket is a longtime employer. If you do, you may find that the eggs you'd hoped would one day turn to gold, have cracked like so many broken dreams.

Loyalty In Moderation

Neil also possesses a healthy skepticism for investing too much of his 401(k) money in his company's stock. His was borne of company loyalty tempered with harsh reality. "If your company requires you to invest your 401(k) money in company stock, you would have no choice," he says. "But if you do have a choice, diversify out of it at the earliest convenience, or as soon as they allow you to do it."

At one time, he felt obliged to put much of his 401(k) money in General Motors stock. He attributes this attitude to the way GM has treated him. "I never asked for a pay raise in my life, and I've gotten many," he says. "They have been very good to me, and they are still being very good to me. That creates loyalty," he adds, "and I still have that loyalty to this day." Even when GM stock took a pounding, he did not stray from this course. He felt the company's treatment of him more than made up for any losses he suffered in his 401(k) plan.

Of course, until the Enron scandal, Neil and his co-workers had little choice; GM required its contribution to employees' 401(k) plans to be invested in company stock. In addition, even after GM changed this policy, he felt a loyal obligation to continue investing the company's contribution in its stock. Once he hired us, in 1994, to manage his plan, he felt fewer obligations to invest or keep his retirement money in GM stock. We also urged him to move most of his money out of GM. We have made sure he is never too exposed to that stock, any other stock, or any other type of investment. "That's why I pay a financial advisor," he says.

He continues to believe that investing in GM is the right thing for him to do. "To invest in your company is like investing in yourself," he says. Having said this, he goes on to urge moderation. "My advice is, yes, invest in your company – it's important," he says.

"But also, diversifying is important as well. You need to strike a healthy balance." Less than 25 percent of his 401(k) plan is in GM stock, a good thing because in late 2006, when he was interviewed for this book, GM stock had taken a nosedive.

Neil thinks he and his GM co-workers have gotten the message from the Enron scandal about the dangers of being too exposed to company stock. "I don't think there's any doubt in anyone's mind," he says. "This could happen at other companies as well."

These days, his 401(k) portfolio is producing excellent results. The plan is worth around $365,000, or three-quarters of all his retirement investments. Several years ago, he paid a six-figure divorce settlement to his former wife. Since then, he has offset the payment through gains in his retirement investments. "It's come back relatively nicely," he says. "Maybe I can retire in five years!"

Neil has a good sense of where to draw the line between company loyalty and his own financial well-being. I expect him to continue behaving this way. I also predict that in five years, when he is 62, he will be living comfortably in retirement.

Tired Of Worrying

While Neil once had much of his 401(k) money in GM stock, Dick at one time had *all* of his 401(k) money in what he calls "The General." As a longtime GM employee, he always thought he should own the company's stock. This was until 2000, when he hired us. He says we set him straight and recalls us telling him then, "This is *your* money and you want your money to work for *you.* If GM stock isn't doing well, let's not own it."

At the time, his 401(k) portfolio consisted almost entirely of stock in GM and Delphi, which GM then owned. Gradually, with our help, he diversified his portfolio into more than a dozen different investments. They are mostly bonds and include some GM stock. One day, Dick asked us why he still had any GM stock in his plan.

"I don't like the way it is going," he said. "I want to dump it all." We followed his command.

"I kept GM stock for the longest time because I felt I owed it to GM to own some of their stock," he now says. "They had been wonderful to me ever since I first walked through their door. They never missed a payday and everything I own I owe to 'The General.' Then I realized it wasn't making me any money. I came to the conclusion that I had asked GM for a job; they didn't ask me to underwrite the company."

Dick also has come to understand the importance of professional financial advice. "If I hadn't hired an advisor, I probably would have ended up staying in two things: GM stock and the GM income fund. I got tired of worrying about the stock market. On bad days I felt terrible, and on good days I felt like I was recovering."

Be More Savvy Than Me

When Bob worked for Lucent, the loyalty bug also bit him. He now advises others to avoid doing likewise. "I wasn't savvy about it and I didn't really care because I thought that was a lifetime job for me," he says. "I started my career with it and was going to retire with it. Lucent encouraged my investment in their stock with the price. They made it really attractive."

He took the bait, partly out of a sense of company loyalty. Another reason: Lucent's stock was booming and it had split several times. "It was company loyalty, and I wanted to see the company succeed," he says. "I tried to encourage other people to take it easy on the company and not beat up on it too badly with overtime and stuff like that."

Bob hopes the rest of us learn from his mistake and diversify our portfolios. "Just be savvy and keep on top of it," he says. "Watch what's going on, and talk to your broker."

He expresses gratitude for the job his one-time advisor, who is now an executive for us, did for him. "He's a great guy," Bob says, "and he was watching out for me."

Common Sense

Unlike Neil and Bob, Carol felt no blind obligation to invest her 401(k) plan in her former employer while she worked there for 30 years. However, she did put some of her retirement money in the stock of the company, AT&T, because the price was right. However, she also never held too much AT&T stock – either while employed there or since the mid '90s, when she went to work for a privately held telecommunications company.

She does not recall exactly how much of her 401(k) plan was in AT&T stock while she worked there. She thinks it was only between 15 and 25 percent. "Everything I've ever read and been told was to diversify," she says. "I've always kept that in mind with my investing."

Carol advises people starting their work and financial careers to follow her example. "Everyone should be diversified. That's just Rule No. 1," she says. "When you look at the big picture, no matter how good a company it is that you're going to be working for, no one is that loyal to you. If the company is giving you its stock, there's a reason for it. Also, you never want to turn down a gift horse."

She is quite pleased with the performance of her 401(k) plan, which is worth about $450,000. Even when the market soars up and then nosedives, she seeks to remain calm. "I try not to get too emotional when I see those peaks and valleys," she says.

From her parents, Carol learned the ethic of saving money. From friends and colleagues she admires, she learned to avoid investing too much of her retirement money in AT&T stock while employed there. "I admire their ethics, financial status, and wisdom. I always pay attention to them and try to learn as much as possible from them," she says. "They told me to diversify," she adds. "It's common sense and made perfect sense to me."

She also realizes she is not a financial-investment expert. "So I didn't allow myself to make all the decisions," she says. "My financial advisor has been very, very good at helping me make the right choices."

Carol is the picture of healthy balance when it comes to her investment strategy. She resists the temptation to invest too heavily in her employer's stock, avoids knee-jerk reactions to fluctuations in the market and saves consistently and understands the value of professional financial advice. I wonder if she'd agree to let us clone her as The Perfect Client?

CHAPTER 5 401(K)NOWLEDGE GAINS

- Ordinarily, limit your company's stock to no more than 10 percent of your portfolio.
- If your company matches your 401(k) contribution in company stock, find out whether you can transfer out of company stock and into some other asset(s).
- Gain your company's support for expanding the investment choices in your plan to these asset classes:
    - Growth-stock mutual funds (large-, mid-, and small-cap stocks).
    - Value-stock mutual funds (large-, mid-, and small-cap stocks).
    - International-stock mutual funds.
    - International-bond mutual funds.
    - Corporate-bond mutual funds.
    - Government-bond mutual funds.
    - Guaranteed-investment contracts.
    - Market-index funds.

6

Reallocate and Rebalance Your Plan's Assets on a Tactical Basis

Presume you will live *forever.*

Did you know that 97 percent of us, once we retire, end up with a lifestyle that is *below* the level of our working years? Young people, in particular, tend to underestimate how long they will live. In this regard, I ask young adults three questions:

1. Did you start saving enough money for retirement as soon as you got out of school?
2. Are you continuing to save and plan enough to achieve your retirement goal?
3. Do you have a methodology to realize your retirement plan?

Most of us – young and old – also neglect a basic, fundamental aspect of managing our 401(k) plan. We fail to reallocate and rebalance our plan's assets on a tactical basis. As I noted in Chapter 1, do not presume you are going to live to, say, age 85, and spend 20 years in retirement. You might actually live to 95 or 105, especially with the continual advances in health and medical care. However, you might also be frail and sickly during many – if not all – of your retirement years. My recommendation: Presume you are going to live *forever* – regardless of the shape you are in – and manage your money accordingly. Then, when you die *before* forever – as we all will do – you will not have outlived your money.

With this in mind, you want to adopt a portfolio-management style that represents a continuum between the passive and the active, as I advised in *The Scarborough Plan: Maximizing the Power of Your 401(k)*:

- **Passive management** means that some system determines which stocks constitute your portfolio. Therefore, hands-on management *per se* is not required. The best example of passive management is index funds, which are designed to mimic the performance of some financial index. A Standard & Poor's 500 index fund, for example, would include the stocks that make up the S&P 500 in amounts reflecting their proportions in this index. Such a fund would require adjustments only as needed to maintain the correct relative amounts of stock required to continue mirroring the S&P 500. An S&P index fund should provide investors the same return they would realize from owning each of the individual stocks in the same proportions – perhaps a bit more or less, depending on the costs and fees – as the weighted index. Therefore, passive management involves managing the logistics instead of selecting the stocks that comprise your portfolio or fund.

- **Active management** means the investor – whether an individual investor or a mutual-fund portfolio manager – selects which stocks to buy and sell according to certain criteria. Actively managed portfolios perform only as well as the stocks that constitute them. Therefore, what the active manager does affects greatly the returns on investments. Active management must combine good stock selection with reasonable turnover – the frequency with which stocks are bought and sold – in order to achieve acceptable returns.

Furthermore, here are several ways you could (but should not) reallocate and rebalance your plan's assets on a tactical basis:

- Use market timing as an "investment" strategy.
- Engage in "day trading."
- Put all of your money into company stock.
- Follow investment tips from "experts" such as your butcher or dry cleaner.
- Ignore your account statements.
- Reallocate and rebalance your assets poorly – or not at all.

While Valerie does not tactically reallocate and rebalance her portfolio as often as she should, Jennifer, Dixie, Kim, Stephanie, and John are much more active in this regard. Kim, Stephanie and John, who are our clients, call us regularly to see how their 401(k) plans are doing. They rely on strategic advice from their investment advisors, coupled with tactical input from themselves, to reallocate and rebalance their plans. They are active *enough* in this regard.

While this might sound like a cop-out, I certainly do not say the same thing about all of my clients.

Here is why: Some clients refuse to discuss their retirement investments with us because it keeps them up at night. Instead, they look at the latest quarterly statements to see whether their account's values has increased, decreased, or remained the same since the last quarter. When it goes up, they are relieved. Then, they put their head in the sand for another 90 days until the next statement arrives – like the ostrich in Chapter 2.

So Far Away

Valerie regards retirement as way off in the distance. However, she does have a general idea of what she wants in the way of life in retirement. "Obviously, I won't be working and, hopefully, I will have enough money saved so that I don't have to work and I can still do the things I enjoy doing," she says. She does not see herself working at all. "That would be lovely," she says,

She admits readily that she has not been an *active* participant in her plan because "it was easier *not* to." She says she has adjusted her portfolio "once or twice." She does not know enough regarding investing, she adds, and learning more about it would require too much of her time and energy. "I keep getting good returns and everything seems to be going okay," she says. "So I'm not doing the research to make sure my allocation is what it should be."

Given her relatively passive participation in her 401(k) plan, she is unwise to assume the plan's manager, an employee of the company for which she works, is closely monitoring it for her. In fairness to Valerie, though, she is the norm in our society. Take a close look at most people who participate in 401(k) plans. The average number of reallocations they make during their entire careers is *zero*.

Instead, they do as Valerie did when she began investing in her 401(k) plan; they decide where to invest their money, and then watch idly to see whether the money grows in the coming years.

At best, they review their investments at least once a year. As long as their portfolio is doing *okay* – that is, not blowing up – they leave it alone.

Overall, Valerie is off to a good start with her 401(k) plan. She put some good thought into her original allocations. Now, she needs to devote more time and energy to reallocating and rebalancing her holdings on a tactical basis. It is important that she do so in order to maintain the style continuity of her portfolio.

Financial Soulmates

Jennifer has a good understanding of the terms "reallocate" and "rebalance" regarding her 401(k) plan. On both counts, she reviews tactically her retirement portfolio when she does her taxes each year. "It's a good time to sit down with your financial advisor to make sure you like the way things are going," she says.

Once, she put her money into a money-market fund, when its monthly interest rate topped 5 percent, instead of her 401(k) plan. Rather than switch the money from the 401(k) into the money market, she directed new savings into the money market. "Reallocation is something I think I will look at every year," she says. "If I see that a particular fund is not going up, I would consider revamping my plan."

Jennifer, a 28-year-old attorney specializing in international-dispute resolution, is particularly fond of international stocks. "Probably," she says, "it's because I was an international business major with a focus on finance." Initially, she pushed her financial advisor to invest her 401(k) money in international stocks. Now, with the resurgence of the U.S. stock markets, she realizes she may need to move some of that money into domestic stocks.

If I did not know any better, I would swear that Jennifer has way too much time on her hands! Seriously, she is refreshing and unusual because she has such a good handle on her 401(k) plan.

My only advice to her: Move from the legal profession to the invest-ment community and make some real money!

Jennifer has a soul mate in Andrew. On the day I talked with him, he had just reallocated and rebalanced his 401(k) plan on a tactical basis. "I do keep track of my 401(k) almost on a daily basis," he says. "I reallocate and rebalance probably every six months."

He does not invest in more than three funds at a time. Usually, it is two. They tend to be a combination of medium-to-high growth and high-risk funds. As you read in Chapter 4, he also displays remarkable financial acumen for his age – or any age, for that matter. In addition, he has a quite healthy approach to his 401(k) plan.

One of the biggest challenges now facing Jennifer and Andrew is the need to maintain a high interest level in their retirement plans, making sure to reallocate and rebalance regularly their portfolios. In short, they cannot take their eyes off their investments because of other issues that will arise in their lives as they get older.

Conscious Decisions

Dixie, 68, thinks she has not done a good enough job reallocating and rebalancing her 401(k) plan on a tactical basis. I disagree with her. "I try to balance my plan between bonds and, even though I am older, a little more risky investments," she says. "I watch the percentage change over the months and years and try to stay away from the investments with minus changes. I must admit that I do not read prospectuses only because I do not have time."

She prefers stocks to bonds because the latter tend to yield less return than the former. She figures 70 percent of her retire-ment plan is in "safer" investments and the other 30 percent in more risky holdings. She has only 15 investment options available through her law firm's 401(k) plan. "So we don't have a whole lot of choice," she says. "I had another plan at another law firm that was totally self-directed. I could go out and buy anything on the open stock market. I used to have a boss and good friend who was a tax partner in the present law firm years ago. I used to show my fund to him and say, 'Does this look okay to you?' I'd go by his advice because he was a lot more savvy investor than I was."

Remember the story in Chapter 2 of the sushi chef and his Japanese workers? We tend to emulate the brightest idiot in the crowd. I am not saying Dixie's friend and former boss was the brightest idiot when he was at her law firm. Instead, I am saying she and the rest of us need to exercise caution with financial advice we receive from people who are not qualified, skilled investment professionals.

Dixie has not made any changes in her 401(k) plan in more than a year. "Things are going well," she says, "so I have seen no reason to change anything." This does not mean she never reallocates and rebalances her plan. Once, her law firm replaced certain investments with others in its 401(k) offerings. She disliked one of the new investment options and did not reallocate any of her retirement money to it. "But that's probably the only reallocation I've done," she says. "I've changed very little since I've been in this 401(k) plan for about 16 years."

What would she do if a mid-cap stock took off? "I probably would not jump in and buy something like that," she answers, "because I know some of those things can go the other way and just totally bottom out." She would not completely ignore such a stock, though. "I would probably read more about it to see whether I could figure out why it's going up like it is," she says. "But I would also be a bit leery because I'm older now and I'm okay with where my plan is."

Dixie has made conscious decisions regarding her 401(k) plan. Clearly, she has a good game plan and follows it well. "I look at my plan a couple times a week," she says. "I also watch the stock market in the newspaper everyday." In this regard, she is head-and-shoulders above most of us. We tend to pick certain investments when we first enter a 401(k) plan and stick mindlessly with them for years on end.

A Reasonable Interest

Kim is also active in the makeup of her 401(k) plan. "I keep an eye on it," she says. I do talk to my advisor probably two to four times a year, I read the statements when they come in, and I read my financial advisor's newsletter. So I take an interest in what is happening. But I wouldn't say I take an *active* interest in terms of suggesting where the money should be invested. I rely on my financial advisor to have that expertise."

More than two decades ago, when she was in her late 20s, she started to look closely at the performance of her 401(k) plan. This motivated her to hire us to manage her plan. "It was a pretty good chunk of change and it was growing," she says. "I decided that if I were not to personally take an active role in managing that money, I should pay somebody to do that."

Kim does not regard herself as a high-risk taker. "I am in some risk funds, and because of my age I can handle that," she says. "But it unnerves me when those funds go up 10 points, then drop 20 points, and then go up 10 points. I don't necessarily want to know about large fluctuations." The frequency of her phone calls to us rose noticeably a few years ago when the high-tech boom came to a crashing halt and blew out the stock market. "I was very concerned at that point," she says. "Basically, my financial advisor told me, 'Chill out. Let it go. It'll come back.' It took a couple of years, but it did come back."

Clearly, she displays a good interest in the makeup and performance of her 401(k) plan. She has done well with her retirement account, which contains a fair amount of money. Moreover, she calls us regularly – but not constantly - to ask why we invested her money in one fund versus another one. As a result, she strikes a proper balance. She knows she needs to have a reasonable interest in the tactical reallocation and rebalance of her 401(k) plan.

Trust Your Advisor

Stephanie also relies heavily on us to reallocate and rebalance her 401(k) plan on a tactical basis. "We talk quarterly," she reports. "I *really* trust my advisor. So when we talk and he tells me what he thinks, I pretty much listen to what he has to say and go with what he advises."

Within the past year, she moved some of her retirement money to Goldman Sachs. She acted on the recommendation of her advisor, who told her this is where his own money is. "I thought, 'Well, he's in the investment business to make money for himself, so I can't be that bad off [following his advice], because my money and his money are in the *same place!*'"

At 64, John is much older than Stephanie. However, they share some investment approaches. He also pays regular attention to the tactical reallocation and rebalance of his 401(k) plan. In addition, he relies heavily on his financial advisor for strategic assistance and guidance.

While he made good money during his working years at GM, he was not a big spender. Toward the end of his career, he traveled considerably as part of his job. Therefore, he lacked much time to spend his money on other things. Frugality is another reason he saved money. He attributes this trait to his upbringing as one of five children of a working-class couple. "I basically came from a poor background," he says. "So I learned how to manage and save money at an early age. There are people who save and people who spend," he adds.

He did not inherit the savings gene from his parents. While they were frugal, they made little money and spent what they did make on vital necessities. "I wanted to learn to save. My dad would come home and give my mother $60 in $20 bills and that was her budget for the week for groceries, clothes and everything else. I'm talking about back in the '50s. If you made $100 a week then, you were doing pretty good."

In John's quest to become a saver, he closely monitors his 401(k) plan. He regularly checks the plan's balance online as well as with his financial advisor by phone. Every month or so, he tracks the plan's performance in a spreadsheet. "We've had some fantastic years!" he says. "From 1995 to 1999, we were getting 20 percent, 30 percent, and 40 percent returns. It was unbelievable!" During his final few years at GM, he contributed as much as $29,000 a year to his 401(k) plan. By the time he retired, in 2001, he had contributed more than $100,000 in *after-tax* money to the plan. He had made this sort of contribution for several years because he had reached the maximum amount of the *pre-tax* contribution for those years. "What better way to save!" he says. "It just sits there and accumulates tax-free on your earnings until you pull it out!"

He retired in 2001 with slightly less than $1 million in his 401(k) and about $50,000 in his IRA. In 2004, on our advice, he rolled the entire 401(k) into a new IRA, which at the time was investing in many more mutual funds than his 401(k) through GM. He also set up irrevocable living trusts. Both moves provided tax advantages for his heirs. These days, he feels comfortable with the way we have reallocated and rebalanced his retirement plan, which is now worth about $1.2 million. "I could pull out of my driveway and get hit by a cement truck tomorrow," he says. "I don't want that money to go to Uncle Sam. I'd much rather have it go to my family."

Stephanie's and John's stories illustrate well an area of retirement planning and investing in which most people tend to err. Such people try to guess whether the financial market is going to rise or fall and where they should enter or exit it. This is why you need to have a specific plan for retirement and then stick to it!

CHAPTER 6 401(K)NOWLEDGE GAINS

- Presume you are going to live *forever* – regardless of the shape you are in – and manage your money accordingly. Then, when you die *before* forever – as we all will do – you will not have outlived your money.

- Start saving for retirement as soon as you get out of school. Continue to save and plan well enough to achieve your retirement goals, and have a methodology to realize these goals.

- When you reallocate and rebalance your retirement portfolio on a tactical basis, rely on strategic advice from your investment advisor coupled with your own tactical input.

- Adopt a portfolio-management style that represents a continuum between the passive and the active.

- Avoid day trading, investing all of your money into company stock, following investment tips from "experts" such as your butcher or dry cleaner, ignoring your account statements, and reallocating and rebalancing your assets poorly – or not at all.

7

Do Not Panic When the Value of Your Plan Declines

The titles of chapters 2 through 11 of this book are the money-management rules we should live by. Of these 10 rules, the hardest one for us to follow is this one: "Do not panic when the value of your plan declines." Why? Simple. It is the only rule that centers entirely on our *emotions*.

This rule is easy to follow once the stock market has rebounded, but not during tough times such as the market decline from 2000 to 2002. It has been only six years since one of the three worst downturns in the stock market's 200 years. When the market does fall, many of us sweat bullets. However, where else can we turn, to invest our money?

As I observed in *The Scarborough Plan: Maximizing the Power of Your 401(k)*, there are no risk-free investments. Period. Sure, you can invest in Treasury bills and be relatively certain that you will get back your principal plus the promised interest. However, can you be sure the interest will be greater than the rate of inflation while you were waiting to get back your money? No. Can you be certain of getting back your entire principal if you need to cash in your T-bill early? Sorry, no. In addition, is there any assurance that you will be able to get the same (or higher) interest rate on the next Treasury bills you buy? No, none. Therefore, when finance types say that T-bills are risk-free, what they really mean is that these notes carry almost no credit risk. Practically speaking, though, your interest-rate risk over the short term is small and you are almost certain to get back your principal. Treasury bills are one of the best places to "store" your money while you are deciding where best to invest it.

Treasury bills aside, we can do little else except put our money in the stock market and ride out the downturns. Doing a good job of practicing this healthy ethic are Greg, John, Gary, Dixie, Andrew, and Jennifer. Ann and Wendy are relatively new to the stock market and have yet to be truly tested. This being said, I can call clients only so many times during a down market and say,

"Trust me, your account *will* go back up" before they get tired of hearing from me.

Intellectually, we know the stock market is prone to ups and downs. It is hard to live with this fact, however, day in and day out, quarter in and quarter out, when our retirement money is on the line. One of the telling signals that we watch for when the stock market slumps, is the number of clients wanting to convert their stock to cash. They cannot viscerally stomach down markets. I am not saying they are right or wrong.

When we receive *many* of these types of phone calls – a half-dozen or more a week as opposed to only one or two weekly – we know more and more of our clients are capitulating. We also know the stock market is close to bottoming out because there are only a limited number of people who cannot – or will not – endure such pain. In short, I see a strong correlation between a sharp increase in clients bailing out of the stock market and the market being near bottom. Usually, the clients who stay in the market and weather the storm do just fine.

Interestingly, once the stock market recovers – as it invariably does – many of the same clients who jumped overboard at or near its bottom claim the market is rigged. Of course, they tend to be the same clients who ask us to convert their cash back to stock. The flipside is when the stock market is near its peak. You would be dumbfounded to know how many of our clients want to throw their retirement money at the top of a market. Anybody who believes he can see a fall or rise coming in the stock market is mistaken. The reality is that none of us – even those of us in the financial investment business – can see one coming.

Don't Ever Get Greedy

Greg hung tough during the stock-market decline of 2001 and 2002. When his 401(k) plan dropped in value, many people said he needed to do something about it; however, he took our advice. "They told me, 'Don't ever get greedy, and don't ever panic,'" he says. "So I sat it out, to see what would happen." Eventually, the value of Greg's portfolio began to head back north. "You have to keep your hands steady on the throttle," he says.

Most corporations send quarterly statements to their employees. It is quite appropriate for those employees to look closely at those statements, to make sure the account is doing what they expect it to do on a long-term basis. This does not mean that you move your money every quarter. Nor does it mean you should have a knee-jerk reaction if your 401(k) plan is treading water or dropping in value. Human nature being what it is, when we see such results, we presume intuitively that we have done something wrong. We think we need to move our money.

As you read in Chapter 6, there are appropriate times to reallocate and rebalance your 401(k) plan. There are also times when you should move all of your plan's assets to another investment vehicle, as John did on our advice three years after his retirement. What should you do when your 401(k) plan continues to tank over several quarters? This is going to seem like an odd answer: If the entire account has been dropping in value at essentially the same rate, and if the portfolio is properly designed for your long-term needs, you could let your account decline for three or four years. This would *not* necessarily mean your funds were improperly invested. However, from a practical viewpoint, it would be a tough ride for you to take.

In fact, from 2000 to 2002, Greg's account lost money while we managed it. I find it tiresome to hear my staff telling clients, "You're doing the right thing, even though you're losing money." Greg is living proof that the best actions you take are the ones you do *not* take. I am not suggesting that you stick your head in the sand. Instead, I am advising you to not panic. By not panicking, you end up making correct decisions. Just let the market do what it does naturally and things will work well for you over the time-frame that fits your situation.

If you sit at your computer trading stocks, you would need to make two correct decisions in order to succeed more often than fail: 1) You would need to sell at the right time; and 2) You would need to buy at the right time. If you were wrong in either case, you would lose money.

As for my own investment portfolio, there have been times when I have thought about firing my own company. Even after being in this business for 25 years, I say to myself now and then, "Has everything I've learned in a quarter-century been flawed?" I know deep down that it has not. Yet, it is tough for me to feel that way when I look at declining values in my latest quarterly statement. On the plus side, this sort of experience puts me in the shoes of my clients and helps me to empathize with them when they live through a similar experience.

Save As Much As You Can

In the immediate aftermath of 9/11, John also saw the value of his 401(k) plan decline significantly. He had retired from General Motors on September 1. "At the time of 9/11, I was newly retired and didn't have that much of a concern, even though my plan took a tremendous hit of almost $300,000," he says. "But within a matter of less than six months, my plan came back at least three-quarters of the way."

He recalls some of his GM colleagues who did not take the big drop in their plans' values as well as he did. "There were people who were actually losing sleep and physically getting sick, and they pulled out of their plans at the bottom and missed the swing when the market went back up," he says. "I go the other way. When stocks are at record highs, that's when I want to go to cash." He adopted that approach after having "ridden that roller-coaster ride down a couple of times." He speaks highly both of our performance and the investment plan we put him in, The Hartford, which sets a floor. "Man, when you have a floor set, you forget about it," John says. "You don't have to worry about it." The Hartford plan would also allow him to reset the base after five years if it has gone up by then. "That's just a fantastic plan," he says.

Despite the tough times that General Motors has experienced in recent years, John is confident that GM's leadership will turn the company around. "I think about the worst-case scenario – General Motors going bankrupt – and whether I want that tension because it would affect my lifestyle," he says. "That's why building your savings while you're still working is so critical. It gives you that little bit of extra security."

Two of his former neighbors in a Florida retirement community, who had worked for United Airlines, were nowhere near as secure. Both of them lost their pensions when the financially struggling United halted all payments to its pension plan in 2004 after it had filed for Chapter 11 reorganization. As a result, the couple had to move to a much smaller, less expensive place up the road. "You say to yourself, 'But for the grace of God, go I,'" John says. "If General Motors ever did go bankrupt and something happened to the pension plan and the executive supplement retirement plan, that's where my savings would become critical. You can't put every-thing at risk."

He feels fortunate that he was able to save enough money for retire-ment. "During my last six or seven years at General Motors, I was saving 15 to 20 percent a year," he says. As a result, he offers sage advice, which he shares with his own children: "Start saving as soon as possible and save as much as you can – especially with the way things are going in corporate America today. Social Security isn't going to be enough to help. It's nice to get that Social Security because it helps to pay the electric bill, but it's not going to cover your greens fees."

Keep Your Cool

Gary is one more of our clients who did not panic when his 401(k) plan declined in the wake of 9/11. His investment portfolio, all of which was in a mutual fund, lost *40 percent*. This caused him much concern post-9/11 because he had put himself on a 10-year timeline toward retirement. However, within four years after the terrorist attacks, his portfolio had returned to its pre-9/11 level.

Today, he is even better protected from the economic ramifications of another disaster. Because of following our advice, he is now spread over stocks and protected investments such as certificates of deposit. "I think if we had another 9/11, I wouldn't be hurt as bad in total," he says. His retirement assets, including his house, are now worth more than $1 million. Overall, he is in great shape. "I attribute a lot of that to my financial advisor – that's why I'm still with them," he says. "They made me be a lot more aware of everything."

I find that, over time, we increase the interest and awareness of our clients regarding their retirement portfolios. Partly, it is because we make a conscious effort to do so. The rest of the time, this tends to occur because the closer our clients get to retirement and the use of their assets, the more interested they become in them. With this heightened interest and awareness, come questions from them and education from us.

The rest, we make a conscious effort to do.

"I Got Over Panic Years Ago."

Dixie responds matter-of-factly when asked whether she ever panics when the stock market takes a big fall. "No," she says. Why not? She laughs. "I got over panic years ago!" the 68-year-old answers. Even when she was much younger, market drops did not upset her. "When you watch the stock market over the years, you see that it goes up and down.

As Dixie told us in Chapter 6, her law firm's 401(k) plan provides only 15 investment options. Therefore, there is not much she can do when the stock market takes a sharp dive. "You can't take what you've got and bail out so that it doesn't get any worse," she says. "But you can reallocate."

As you also read in Chapter 6, I think she does a good job of real-locating and rebalancing her 401(k) plan on a tactical basis. You might say that she comes by her steel nerves naturally. Her father did fairly well at investing in the stock market. "My Dad used to say, 'Don't sweat the small stuff. It'll all be the same in 100 years,'" she says. "He rode any wave that came along without panicking." While she may keep her panic in check whenever the stock market dips precipitously, she does feel genuine concern. "I always wonder when or if it's going to go back up again," she says.

Dixie possesses a healthy view of her retirement money and an excellent approach to looking at it on a long-term basis. These traits appear to be borne of her upbringing. Indeed, I do not think we are born with them.

He Ought to Be Working for Me

Andrew, 28, is quite pragmatic about the ups and downs of the stock market. When the stock market falls, his first instinct is to remain calm. "I look back at the last 90 years and see the market goes through changes and rebounds," he says. "I understand that it's not going to continue to go up. If it did, everyone would be millionaires by now." He cannot touch the money in his 401(k) plan, without suffering financial penalties, until he is 59½. "So my plan has a long way to go," he says.

He did not have a 401(k) plan when 9/11 occurred. "I might have had a different feeling," he says. "But I haven't had any major drops like the market had back then." He has the right attitude about stock market declines. He has a good methodology for saving and investing toward retirement. He ought to be working for me!

Adhering to the Latte Effect

Jennifer is also relatively young. She has been in the stock market long enough, though, to ride a roller-coaster ride of decline and recovery. A few years ago, the two mutual funds she first bought when she was 16 lost money. "It did catch my breath – especially at that time," she says. "I was still in school and I didn't have a lot of extra money. When you're living on $2,000 a semester and you lose $100, that's a lot of money," she adds. "That was 5 percent of my money just going away!"

Her initial reaction: "Oh, good God, we need to do something." Her secondary reaction, after a good night's sleep: the damage is already done. "I'm a big fan of looking at the three-, five- and ten-year trends," she adds. "I've seen where, in the past, there have been little dips. I saw them as normal." She did not panic. Instead, she kept her money in the funds, hoping she would recover the lost money once the stock market rose again. She responded exactly as I would have liked her to. She left the funds alone and, when the stock market came back, her funds did, too.

Jennifer did not inherit a knack for shrewd investing from her parents, despite the fact that they have owned successful small businesses since she was two years old. "They do a fantastic job at running small businesses," she says. "But the value of their retirement funds is about equivalent to mine, because I put so much into it every year." At some point in her life, she may need to care for her parents. She feels her upbringing has well prepared her to handle such a big responsibility. "I've always been into putting my money away and watching it grow," she says. "I don't necessarily need the new Coach handbag."

She admits to spoiling herself on occasion with luxury purchases. She insists, however, that she usually adheres to the "latte effect." That is, she forsakes small, daily indulgences and invests the money she would have spent on them in her 401(k) plan instead. If she continues with this behavior over the long haul, her plan will generate large amounts of compounded interest. For her, the compounded interest should more than offset all of the large and small dips the stock market will take between now and then.

Feeling the Way He Should at His Age

In the five years since Omar began his 401(k) plan, he has seen the stock market decline significantly. He has yet to panic. "There are going to be some storms," he says, "and there are going to be some nice days." He developed this healthy attitude on his own. "I did a lot of reading about the stock market," he says. "I also looked at the market to see how it reacts and how people react or over-react to it."

He is 35, so he will be in his 401(k) plan for at least another 25 years. "I'm not going to worry at this time," he says. "As I get older, that will change. If I get married, I will be less risky and aggressive than I am now."

Fast forward to 2030, when Omar will be 58. If the stock market is quite volatile then, I am sure he would feel differently than he does now. Currently though, he feels the way he should at his age. If he becomes more conservative with age and adjusts accordingly his 401(k) plan, it would be a smart move. The problem is that typical Americans make no changes in their 401(k) plans during their entire working careers.

I am not saying Omar is going to do this. However, let us say he were to continue working for the federal government for the next 25 years, and the only thing he does with his 401(k) plan is to continue putting money in it at his current rate of investment. He could potentially have an extremely volatile retirement account. In short, he will have the roller-coaster ride from hell!

A Good Test for Her

Ann has been in her 401(k) plan for only two years. During this time, she has not experienced much volatility in the stock market. When she does encounter her first volatile market, she believes it will be a good test for her. "I believe I will stay cool," she says. "I do believe that's why I did choose to invest very aggressively." She is consciously aware of the cyclical nature of the stock market. "My mother has been investing her entire adult life," she says. "I've been listening to her and watching CNBC with her – she has it on all day."

At least one thing does worry Ann, though. In saving and investing for retirement, she is behind where she should be for her age. During each of the first two years in her 401(k), she has invested the maximum amount allowed by the plan. "I'm looking everywhere I can to get caught up," she says.

If you wait too long to begin catching up, it could be difficult for you to do so successfully. However, you would have little choice but to make the effort even though you may need to work well beyond the age at which you now plan to retire. Either that, or get a new job that pays a lot more money!

Intellectually Prepared, Emotionally Unsure

Wendy, 35, has been in a 401(k) plan for only five years. It is long enough, though, for her to have learned to remain calm when the stock market declines markedly and recovers slowly. "When I go to meetings with our 401(k) plan manager, they always tell us to think of our investments in the long run," she says. "We can't look at it just in the short term."

She has yet to experience a steep drop in the stock market, but she says she is intellectually prepared for one. Is she ready emotionally for her first roller-coaster ride? "I'm not sure," she responds. She describes herself as "more of a cautious person." Some people withstand the downward ride by closing their eyes and not looking. Others keep their eyes open, aware the ride will head upward again, and continue investing money in their 401(k) plans.

I am 100 percent certain that Wendy will eventually take the downward ride. The question is: Will she be able to withstand the pain? She does not think she will panic. "I have not made any changes in my plan over the past four years," she says. "I'm not sure that will change if I start seeing it lose money." This could turn out to be true. Even if it does, I expect she would much more frequently check the status of her portfolio than she does now.

It is human nature to react in a knee-jerk way. You begin to wonder whether you are making mistakes. You also ask more questions than before. I encourage you to call your financial advisor whenever you have these sorts of doubts and questions. Occasionally, it is quite appropriate to ask your advisor to essentially hold your hand and tell you everything is going to be okay.

CHAPTER 7 401(K)NOWLEDGE GAINS

- Treasury bills aside, you can do little else except put your money in the stock market and ride out the downturns.

- It is nearly impossible to see a fall – or rise – coming in the stock market, so avoid a knee-jerk reaction to market volatility.

- When the stock market does precipitously plummet, ask your financial advisor for assurance that the market – and your plan – will eventually recover.

- As you get closer to retirement, become more conservative with your investments in order to help soften the blow of volatility in the financial markets.

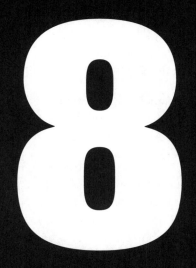

8

Know Your Plan's Options and Features

Be well-prepared to ask all the right questions.

As we have learned from Bob, ignorance is *not* bliss. This is true in general. It is especially true regarding the options and features of your 401(k) plan. All John really lacked was the skill to monitor the performance of his plan, including its options and features. Once he hired us, he considerably reduced his stress level.

Beth knows most of the fine minutiae of her plan. Because she is in her mid-30s, she has plenty of time to learn the rest. Kim and Jennifer also know their plans inside and out, while Andrew is sophisticated and perceptive about the options and details of his plan.

Wendy knows more than most people about the options and features of her 401(k) plan. However, she has much more to learn. Omar, on the other hand, is quite unaware of the options and features of his plan and can either take a crash course or hire a financial advisor. These are the only two choices he has.

Federal law establishes features that 401(k) plans *may* (but not *must*) have, as I noted in *The Scarborough Plan: Maximizing the Power of Your 401(k)*. You would like your plan to have all the options and features allowed by law, whether or not you actually use them. The greater the number of options and features your plan has, the greater the flexibility you will have in managing your 401(k) assets to your advantage.

The options and features that are most common and most desirable are as follows:

- Loan provisions.
- Matching contributions.
- After-tax contributions.
- Immediate eligibility.
- Investment advice.
- Investment style.
- Separate record keeper and fund manager.

- Daily valuations.
- Voice-response units.
- Unlimited allocation changes.

When you meet with your company representative to size up your 401(k) plan, make sure you are well prepared to ask all the right questions. The best approach is to take the checklist, below, along with you. Check off the features and services offered by your plan and ask about the ones not offered. Since no two plans are alike, you should consider the following priorities:

Priority One

- Eligibility is immediate.
- Wide range of investment alternatives is available (15 to 20, or more).
- Company match is reasonable. (Dollar for dollar is best; 50 percent, up to 6 percent of gross income, or more is acceptable.)
- Investment advice is available.

Priority Two

- Vesting period is reasonable. (Immediate is best; 20 percent or more annually is acceptable.)
- Employee directs investment of company match.
- Maximum contribution permitted is at least 15 percent.
- Daily valuations are done.

Priority Three

- Loan provisions are acceptable.
- The number of allocation changes is unrestricted.
- Voice-response capability exists.

Priority Four

- Pre- and post-tax contributions are permitted.
- In-service withdrawals are allowed.
- Separate record keeper and fund manager exist.

Once you have completed the checklist, you will be able to determine how well your 401(k) plan measures up. Generally speaking, the more boxes you have checked, the better the plan will be for you. If only a small number of boxes are checked, the plan may be seriously flawed. However, the number of checked boxes is not as important as *which* boxes are checked. Voice-response units (Priority Three), for example, would be nice. On the other hand, a wide range of investment alternatives (Priority One) would be essential.

Removing Stress and Worry

When John began at GM in 1965, he lacked the skills to manage the savings on which he planned to retire. However, he had the good sense to save as much money as he could for retirement. Many years later, he realized he needed help dealing with the various options and details of his 401(k) plan. Therefore, he hired a financial advisor

In the mid '80s, GM gave only a handful of 401(k) investment options to its employees. John made his choices based strictly on performance over the long term. He also never invested in more than five or six funds at a time. GM did not provide internal or external resources to rank-and-file employees to help them choose the best options. However, the company did offer such assistance to certain high-level executives who needed help avoiding unnecessary taxes on their stock options. "General Motors always took a very conservative approach and did not make investment recommendations to all employees," he says. "If they had, and the investments did not perform well, the employees would have held them responsible."

A few years later, though, GM made outside financial advisors available to all employees who require help managing their 401(k) plans. In 1994, John hired us to manage his retirement plan. At the time, GM's employee-investment plans had several more investment options than when he began with the company nearly 30 years earlier. Back then, he thought to himself, "I work hard like everyone else. I don't have a lot of time to analyze and try to determine where to put my money. With all the different options, it's kind of a shot in the dark unless I really want to do some research."

John attended a presentation I made to GM employees in 1994. As he listened, he thought, "Here's a guy who's got some research going on and is talking about how to set up a managed, balanced account." He says he and a co-worker, who also became a client of ours, agreed to "let the experts do their thing. All we needed to do was monitor the performance of our plans. If we didn't like the performance, we could always go in another direction. It took a lot of the stress and worry away from making investment decisions."

John's experience is quite typical of what we find usually when we make presentations to a company's employees. Most people prefer to let a professional financial advisor handle their retirement money. As I like to say, "They are looking for the *smarter idiot.* I guess they view us as being the smarter idiot." Hmm, perhaps I should use that as our slogan!

The Fine-Tuning Stuff

Ann believes she has good enough knowledge of her 401(k) plan's options and features. She hesitates, however, when she says this: "I definitely understand the fund choices," she says. "But I don't know my way around our law firm's 401(k) plan's website that well." She has reallocated her retirement portfolio at least once. "But I'm not familiar with how that really works," she says. "Certainly, I need to know some of the fine-tuning stuff."

Her law firm recently made financial advisors available to its employees. The federal Pension Protection Act, which became law in 2006, allows companies to provide this sort of service to its workers. "They started sending us a lot of literature, letting us know about that option," she says. "I have not used it yet." She does not expect to use it, either. At least, not while she is with her present employer. "I'll be here only a few more months," she says. "So I'm not terribly concerned about learning all the ins and outs of my plan." She intends to learn those details once she lands another job elsewhere.

Ann is quite typical in this regard. Our 401(k) plan is most likely the one financial vehicle that will determine how well or poorly we live in retirement. Yet I am amazed to find that most of us lack adequate understanding of either our plans' details or the process required to adjust them. People should know the fine minutiae of their retirement plans, including the limitations. Having said this, Ann has 90 percent of what she needs to know. She is 37 and has enough time to learn the other 10 percent. At her age, what she does not know about her 401(k) plan is not going to come back and bite her.

I find often that people say they will learn more about their retire-ment portfolio *later*, not *now*. While Ann says she will learn the parameters of her plan in her next job, she has been in the work-force for many years. She should already know them! It is easy for us to kid ourselves into believing this is something we will do tomorrow. Yet when tomorrow rolls around, we tend to put it off again until the next tomorrow. Don't wait until next time because there is no next time! It's right now!

Not the Norm

Kim knows the high-level details of her 401(k) plan. That is, how much of her money she has invested in each type of fund. However, she lets us manage these details for her. "I'm pretty happy with them," she says of us.

At one point in her 28-year career with the Bell System, she worked in the payroll department of AT&T. "I was amazed at the number of managers who did not participate in the 401(k) plan – even with the company's matching funds," she says. "In most cases, I found that I could increase my contribution on a pre-tax basis. In some cases, I would see an increase in my paycheck. It wasn't much – a couple dollars here and there. I never understood why other people wouldn't participate in the plan – even at 1, 2, or 3 percent."

Kim is selling herself a bit short. When she hired us more than 20 years ago, she knew exactly how much she needed to invest in her

401(k) plan to qualify for the company match from AT&T. She invested this amount, and did so on a pre-tax basis. She also knew her plan's assets had grown to become *real* money. Yet she agreed to let us manage it for her. Since then, she has participated actively in her plan. She has also regularly increased her contributions in order to achieve her retirement goal.

Unfortunately, this sort of behavior is not the norm. Many years ago, I conducted a survey at AT&T – then, one of my client companies – to determine the participation rates for the company's 401(k) plan. If you think higher-paid employees saved and invested more of their paychecks for retirement, you would be mostly wrong. My finding: There was little correlation between *pay* level and *participation* level.

Kim is one of the few people who had her eyes and ears open from day one of her saving-and-investment history. In fairness to everyone else though, this is why they hire financial advisors like us to worry about the options and features of their 401(k) plans. If financial advisors did not exist, what would this second group of people do instead? It makes you wonder.

Warm And Fuzzy

Jennifer also knows her plan's features inside-out. "I definitely try to know them," she says. "I think that everyone could do better at that." She has not always been this way. "At the end of the '90s, when my 401(k) plan took a hit, I didn't know what was going on," she says. "Immediately, I began looking for my annual statements."

She closely examined the industries she had invested in and the people running the companies in those industries. "They looked like very successful people who had had great businesses," she says. "It made me feel better – I had a warm and fuzzy feeling."

Jennifer goes a step further than most people do. She tries to patronize the businesses in which her 401(k) plan is invested. "If a mutual fund contains, say, BP stock instead of Shell stock, there's something to be said when I need gas and see a BP station and a Shell station across the street from each other," she says. "I make sure *my* gas station gets the profit and not another one. You can make a difference in your investment by doing little things like that," she adds. "Especially, if everyone does it." I think what Jennifer says is very true.

Sophisticated And Savvy

As a boy two decades ago, Andrew developed an intimate knowledge and awareness of the stock market by watching and learning from his uncles. "Now, I get e-mails from them daily on the stock they're playing," he says. From his uncles, he learned about the factors that make the stock markets move, including economic and earnings reports. He also learned much from a financial-planning and financial-management course he took while obtaining his MBA. He has been practicing what his uncles preach for the last six years and what he learned in the classroom since he graduated from college. These days, in addition to conversing regularly with his uncles he also watches many of the financial shows on TV.

Andrew, who makes a good living with Cardinal Health, regards playing the stock market as "a great way to earn a second income." He uses some of this income to continue playing the market. Some he spends on his children and some he puts in his 401(k) plan. I find Andrews's knowledge of saving and investing toward retirement to be amazing. He is equally sophisticated and perceptive about the options and details of his 401(k) plan. As I noted (Chapter 4), he is certainly out of the ordinary, especially given his age. I think it is pretty tough for most people of Andrew's age to behave as he does in this regard.

Much More To Learn

As we have seen (Chapter 4), Wendy does not know the options and features of her 401(k) plan well enough. Ironically, her company recently chose her on a random basis to participate in a quarterly audit of the firm's 401(k) plan. "I did actually ask people in my office about our plan's options and details," she says. She had to complete a survey form listing her holdings and asking whether the information about each one was correct. "I had to answer that I did not know," she says, "because I haven't looked at the plan in detail since 2003." This was when she joined the plan. "A lot of other people in my office felt the same way," she adds. "They don't know much about their plan, either."

Sadly, what Wendy knows about her 401(k) plan is typical of most people saving and investing for retirement. However, she does know how much of her paycheck she invests pre-tax in her plan. She also knows how much of this amount her company matches. And she knows how to switch her retirement money from one fund to another. In this regard, she is ahead of most other people regarding knowledge of options and features. Still, the answers she gave on that survey form show she has much more to learn.

Unfamiliar With Too Much

Then there is Omar. He knows the types of funds in his 401(k) plan, but is unfamiliar with too many of the plan's details. "I think I know the basics," he says. "But I'd really like to know more about my 401(k) plan and approach it in a much better way." He joined the Treasury Department's 401(k) plan six years ago. He feels he has learned more about it each year since. His plan is now worth $30,000, which he regards as a small amount of money. This is quite normal for people with 401(k) plans. If he continues to save and invest well, he could eventually see ten times as much in his 401(k) plan. I suspect he would regard $300,000 as a large sum of money.

Omar has one of two choices to make regarding his retirement plan: 1) spend considerable time and energy studying the stock market and his plan's holdings; or 2) hire a financial advisor to manage his retirement money for him. If he does the former, he would realize his lack of knowledge could seriously hurt him.

Should he choose option two, his 401(k) plan could generate much more money for his retirement years. For his sake, I hope he does the latter as soon as possible.

CHAPTER 8 401(K)NOWLEDGE GAINS

- Generally, the more options and features your company's plan has, the greater the flexibility you have to manage your assets to your advantage.

- The most common, desirable options and features are: loan provisions; matching contributions; after-tax contributions; immediate eligibility; investment advice; investment style; separate record keepers and fund managers; daily valuations; voice-response units; and unlimited allocation changes.

- Know the options and features that your company's plan offers and ask about the ones it does not offer.

- Consider the four sets of priorities to determine whether the options and features are reasonable and acceptable to you.

- The number of priority items available is not as important as *which* priority items are available.

9

Consider the Tax Consequences of Your Actions

The great comedian Arthur Godfrey once said, "I'm proud to pay taxes in the United States. The only thing is, I could be just as proud for half the money." If you are going to minimize the sums you hand over to Uncle Sam (proudly or not), you need to consider *all* the tax consequences of your actions regarding your 401(k) plan.

Like all of us who have yet to reach 59½, Wendy has no way of knowing what her tax burden will be when she turns this age and begins withdrawing money from her plan. This is one of the most critical 401(k) issues facing us. Omar and many other younger people face another pressing question: Should they invest their retirement money in a 401(k) or a Roth IRA? The answer is quite elusive.

For Kim, "elusive" is not in her vocabulary. She even understands the workings of 72(t), an obscure but valuable section of federal tax law regarding retirement plans. And, if only there were more Dixies in the world, teaching people about the tax consequences of their 401(k) actions would be much easier. She is a legal secretary to a tax attorney.

However, even if we lack tax-law background and experience, we could still do a better job of protecting our retirement plan from the taxman. Andrew, who has financial skills and abilities, is an excellent example for us to follow. Ann lacks sophisticated knowledge of financial investment and tax law. Still, she has a good basic understanding of the tax implications of her 401(k) actions. Tax law is not Jennifer's bailiwick. Therefore, she relies on financial advisors and online searches to avoid tax problems.

As I wrote in *The Scarborough Plan: Maximizing the Power of Your 401(k)*, you need to protect your money from Uncle Sam – legally. First, we need to distinguish between qualified and non-qualified retirement plans. Qualified plans include defined pension plans, defined contribution plans such as the 401(k) and 403(b) and profit-sharing plans. These plans qualify for various tax advantages by satisfying the relevant provisions of the Internal Revenue Code.

For all the money you invest pre-tax into a qualified plan (plus all the money *that* money earns), you will not pay taxes until you begin making withdrawals years down the road.

Non-qualified retirement plans – formal and informal – include all the rest. They do not receive the same protection against income taxes as qualified plans do. Income is invested into non-qualified plans post-tax – after you have already paid taxes on the money you invested. On top of this, you will be taxed on the earnings of these investments. Personal savings suffer the same fate as non-qualified plans. They also represent post-tax dollars and their earnings – interest, dividends and capital gains – are taxed each year.

One of your goals must be to avoid these taxes for as long as *legally* possible. Why? Because you will be able to build your retirement package bigger and faster by using every penny right from the start. Consider this example of how qualified plans can enable your investments to grow much faster than non-qualified plans or personal savings. You have $2,000 to put aside each year, you are in the 28 percent federal income tax bracket and the 5 percent bracket for your state. You have found an investment that will return 7.5 percent annually year in and year out for the near future. This represents a conservative estimate, given the long-term average annual return of 8.5 percent provided by stocks. Take a look at the difference in value reached by money invested pre-tax in a qualified plan compared to investments that do not offer deferred taxation. Clearly qualified plans – simply by avoiding taxes – out run normally taxed income in no time.

Real Rate of Return			
At the end of the year	Your qualified plan will have	Your taxed plan will have	A difference of
1	$2,150	$1,407	$743
2	$4,461	$2,885	$1,576
5	$12,488	$7,780	$4,708

Real Rate of Return (cont.)			
At the end of the year	Your qualified plan will have	Your taxed plan will have	A difference of
10	$30,416	$17,772	$12,694
15	$56,154	$30,425	$25,729
20	$93,105	$46,658	$46,447
25	$146,152	$67,400	$78,752
30	$222,309	$93,904	$128,405

These figures do not take into account the fact that many employers match some of your investment with a contribution of their own into your qualified plan – a match that also grows tax-deferred!

You should be able to take home two messages from this example:

1. Invest as much as you are permitted in your qualified plan in order to maximize your retirement account's growth and ultimate value.

2. As much as possible, invest your retirement savings first in vehicles such as IRAs that provide similar tax advantages to those of 401(k) and 403(b) plans.

Wendy knows she contributes pre-tax dollars to her 401(k) plan. She is also aware she could face taxes and penalties if she withdraws money from her plan before she is 59½ and does not roll the funds into another 401(k) or an IRA. However, she is unsure of the tax burden she will face when she starts taking money from her plan at age 59½. Unfortunately, most of us lack this critical piece of knowledge. "Now I need to find out how I will be taxed when I retire," she says upon hearing this. "I'm sure it won't be as much as the 30 or 40 percent rate I'd be taxed if I took money out before then, for a vacation."

At least Wendy understands she can withdraw money from her retirement plan, penalty-free, to purchase a house as a first-time homebuyer. She also knows she will have a certain amount of time to repay the money to her plan without suffering tax penalties. When you withdraw early from your plan, the money is taxed as unearned income, although you do not face FICA and Social Security withholdings. You also pay a 10 percent penalty unless you are either at least 59½ or making a qualified purchase such as a house. Furthermore, the state and federal taxes you need to pay would be at the prevailing rates. During Word War Two, for example, the maximum marginal federal tax rate peaked at 94 percent to support the war effort.

Say you will be 59½ in two years. You sense the tax rates are going to zoom way up between now and then because of mounting domestic and international troubles. What should you do? Stop putting money in your 401(k) plan. Invest the funds instead in a Roth IRA, which requires you to pay taxes on the money *before* you invest it. Then, when you begin to withdraw the money at 59½, you will do so tax-free. You can look up to two years ahead for likely tax rates…but not much further than that. Remember that Congress and state legislatures can change tax laws at any time. So following tax laws and regulations is like playing Monopoly when the rules shift regularly. These tax laws and regulations are moving targets, which makes it difficult for you to plan on a long-term basis for what the tax rates may be once you are ready to use your retirement funds.

Facing A Conundrum

Omar has never taken money from his 401(k) plan. Nor does he plan to do so. He is quite aware he could face financial penalties should he withdraw money before he is 59½. He is saving to buy a house and has a Roth IRA in addition to a 401(k). Because he paid taxes up front on the money he invested in the IRA, he will not need to pay additional taxes once he withdraws this money. For his eventual house purchase, he chose between investing in a 401(k) and a Roth IRA. His selection illustrates the defining question about our federal and state tax laws. Do we put our retirement

money, tax-*deferred*, in a 401(k) and watch it grow tax-*deferred*?
Or do we invest these funds, *after*-tax, in a Roth IRA and see the
money grow tax-*free*?

Omar and many young people face this pressing question. There
is no correct answer. The reason: None of us knows what the tax
rates will be when we ultimately withdraw money from our retirement plan. It would be nice if we could put half our retirement
eggs in the 401(k) basket and the other half in the Roth IRA basket
within the *same* retirement plan. The problem is that federal law
does not allow many of us to run our henhouse this way. We need
to choose one or the other.

In Omar's case, he has a 401(k) at work and a Roth IRA on his
own. Federal tax law allows him to have both because his annual
income is low enough. He earns $62,000 a year, which is well below
his threshold of $110,000. However, he still needs to pay income
taxes on the money he invests in the IRA. When we are young,
single and paying rent, we lack the ability to take tax deductions.
Therefore, Uncle Sam taxes our paycheck heavily.

Therefore, Omar may be better off investing his retirement money
in the 401(k). If he does so, he would reduce his taxable income.
Once he buys a house, he could put any new retirement savings into
the IRA instead of the 401(k). The new money would then grow
tax-free. This is the long-term upside. The long-term downside:
He does not know what the tax rate will be when he is 59½ and he
might need to withdraw money from his plan then.

By definition, people who are decades away from being able to
withdraw money from their 401(k) plan penalty-free are at a big
disadvantage. Compared to people who will be 59½ in a year or
two, they have a much fuzzier idea of what the tax rates will be
once they reach this age. As a result, Omar debates whether to roll
his IRA money into his 401(k) plan and redirect all new contributions into the latter. "I'm confused as to what I should do," he says.
He says it well and he faces a real conundrum. At some point,

he and the rest of us will need to make intelligent *guesses* and live with the results!

I do not want it to appear that the answer to everything is for you to hire a financial advisor. In this case, you just need to be smart about what you do with your retirement funds. This requires you to ask a lot of questions and do a lot of reading. Hopefully, this will enable you to make the correct decisions much more often than not.

Well Prepared to Solve the Riddle

Kim has also invested her retirement money in a 401(k) plan on a pre-tax basis. She, too, encounters the same riddle as Omar. However, she is well prepared to solve it. The proof is the success she has had with her retirement investments over nearly three decades. "Some of it, I learned over the years from experience," she says. "Some of it, I learned from asking questions. I think I've had just about every type of IRA plan there is just because of time, tax rules and situations. A lot of my success comes from just asking questions and having someone reliable that I can ask."

She turned 50 in the past year. At that time, she increased her contribution to her 401(k) plan. "I look at it basically as pushing out my tax exposure to when my income is going to be less," she says. "The more money I can keep and not give to the government, the better off I'll be." For most of us, our eyes glaze over when we contemplate the tax consequences of our retirement-investment decisions. Not Kim. She finds the time and energy to gain a good understanding of the impact of tax laws. She gives her retired father a large amount of the credit for her success.

She even understands how the little-known 72(t) plan works. A 72(t) allows you to take money from your 401(k) and IRA at any age without incurring the 10 percent penalty tax for early with-drawal. Once you start removing money, however, you cannot stop until two things happen: you have withdrawn money for at least five consecutive years; and you are at least 59½. A free 72(t) calculator is available at *www.dinkytown.net/java/Retire72T.html.*

The 72(t) is an often misunderstood but also very important part of the federal tax code. This is especially true when you retire and take distributions prior to 59½, which a significant minority of people tend to do.

Knows All the Rules

Dixie is very familiar with the tax laws inside and out. As a legal secretary for a tax attorney, she has gained a solid understanding of tax issues around her plan. She is like a good athlete; she knows all the rules. This is quite unusual. I interviewed 20 people for this book. Only a small handful knew all the provisions of their 401(k) plan and how those work; Dixie was one of them. I wish more of us possessed her legal knowledge and experience regarding 401(k) plans.

Not all of us are tax attorneys or their legal secretaries. Still, we do not need to be in a law practice to learn how to cope with the tax consequences of our actions regarding our 401(k) plan. Take Andrew. He has adopted an "out of sight, out of mind" philosophy regarding the money in his retirement plan. "I've gotten used to living without the money I've put into the 401(k)," he says."

Not all of us are as disciplined. Some of us withdraw money early from our retirement plan. As a result, we suffer tax consequences. "I think the reason people withdraw early when they have a financial crisis," he says, "is that they don't adjust their lifestyle according to what they're putting in their 401(k)." Andrew could not be more correct.

Ann is not as skilled and experienced as Andrew at managing a 401(k) plan. However, she has a good understanding of how her actions affect her tax exposure. "I know the interaction between the tax savings you are getting by putting money in the 401(k)," she says, "and how that affects the income tax that you pay at the end of the year." By packing away money on a pre-tax basis, she is doing the right thing. She needs to continue with this behavior.

Would Rather Eat Ramen Noodles

Sarcastically, Jennifer says her favorite word is "taxes." As a result, she considers "absolutely" the tax consequences of her actions regarding her 401(k) plan. "The most important thing I've done is to put the maximum amount allowed in my 401(k)," she says. She refers to a popular, cheap dish that many financially struggling people dine on. "I would rather eat Ramen noodles than not max out my plan," she says, "because maxing out is one of the best ways to save my money from being taxed."

While Jennifer is not a tax attorney, she has taken a course in tax law. She does not claim, however, to be an expert in this legal area. Nevertheless, she understands better than most of us how to decipher the legal jargon in tax laws and regulations. That said, she relies on her accountant to calculate her taxes when they meet once a year. "I tend to think throughout the year in terms of investment strategy," she says, "not the filing of the taxes."

When she has a tax question between annual visits with her accountant, she does not call the accountant. Instead, she goes online. In recent years, the federal government allowed us to invest an additional amount of pre-tax money a year in our 401(k) plans. Jennifer did a Google search to find out when the change took place and how long it will be in effect. "Nowadays with the Internet, there's just so much information out there," she says. "The IRS website has some great tools on tax consequences."

The IRS web address is *www.irs.gov*.

What if you are not an attorney – never mind one who specializes in taxes? Jennifer thinks everyone should still be able to understand most of the information posted on general websites regarding tax laws and regulations. "Attorneys have a tendency to limit themselves to legal websites such as LexisNexis and West Law," she says. "However, the general public and business people tend to use Google as a first resource." What if we *are* confused by what we read online? Simple, she says. Ask your accountant about it. "I know that if I hadn't maxed out my 401(k) or hadn't bought a house, given my income level," she adds, "my accountant would have asked me why I hadn't done that."

You can also use an online calculator to determine the tax consequences of actions with your 401(k) plan. The websites of many banks and investment companies contain this handy tool, which is easy for you to use on your own. A free 401(k) calculator is available at *www.dinkytown.net/java/Retire401k.html*.

CHAPTER 9 401(K)NOWLEDGE GAINS

- Qualified plans include defined pension plans, defined contribution plans such as the 401(k) and 403(b), and profit-sharing plans. These plans qualify for various tax advantages by satisfying the relevant provisions of the Internal Revenue Code.

- Non-qualified retirement plans – formal and informal – include all the rest. They do not receive the same protection against income taxes as qualified plans do. Income is invested into non-qualified plans post-tax and you are taxed on the earnings of these investments.

- Personal savings also represent post-tax dollars and their earnings are taxed each year.

- Avoid these taxes for as long as *legally* possible because you will be able to build your retirement package bigger and faster by using all of your invested money right from the start.

- Invest as much as you are permitted in your qualified plan in order to maximize your retirement account's growth and ultimate value.

- As much as possible, invest your retirement savings first in vehicles such as IRAs that provide similar tax advantages to those of 401(k) and 403(b) plans.

10

Balance Your Need for Both Income and Growth When Allocating Your Plan's Assets

Get a clue.

Too many of us, as I have noted (Chapter 2), stick our heads in the sand when it comes to our 401(k) money. Once a year, we pull out our heads to see how our retirement funds are doing. We are clueless about balancing our need for both income and growth when we allocate our plan's assets. We need to get a clue.

Wendy has one. Eyeing her retirement in a few decades, she realizes her money will need to continue growing, once she does retire, to counter inflation. Stephanie knows she needs to strike a healthy balance between income and growth once she is retired. However, she has no idea what that balance will need to be then. Ann is young enough to seek growth instead of income. Nevertheless, she – and almost everyone else I profiled in this book – needs to figure out how long she expects to live in retirement so she will not outlive her money. Omar, Valerie, Andrew and Jennifer have put much of their retirement monies in stocks. They are not worried because they know their funds should more than recover any losses by the time they retire many years from now.

In both Chapter 4 and *The Scarborough Plan: Maximizing the Power of Your 401(k),* I outlined the three types of retirement portfolios, based on how far from (or close to) needing cash flow from your plan you are.

- **Aggressive growth.** You are more than 12 years away.
- **Moderately aggressive growth.** You are between 5 and 12 years away.
- **Fairly conservative growth.** You are within 5 years away.

As I also advised in *The Scarborough Plan,* you need a cash-flow figure to determine how much principal you will need to have invested for your retirement. To arrive at this figure, take your current monthly (or annual) income, increase it by 3 percent for inflation, and compound it annually for every year between now and when you will need the cash flow. Here is a table that does this for you for a selected number of years. Multiply the values in the table by the amount you think you will need for a given period.

How long until I need the money	How much I will need per $1,000 in today's dollars
1 years	$1,030
3 years	$1,093
5 years	$1,159
10 years	$1,344
15 years	$1,558
20 years	$1,806

Remember that this represents income, not savings. The point here is that you will likely need the same number of dollars after you retire as you need now – adjusted for inflation. If anyone suggests otherwise, ask them how you will reach all of your retirement goals by spending less money in retirement than you live on today.

Furthermore, planning to die broke is unwise for at least two reasons. First, it ignores all those for whom you care and who may outlive you. Second, planning to die broke requires that you die at precisely the right time. Your only reasonable alternative, therefore, is to plan as though you are going to live forever. By doing so, you will plan to live solely off the income generated by your investments and not off the principal amount itself. This approach assures that you will have a perpetual income and that money will be left over for your heirs when you actually do die.

Over a long investment horizon – say five years or so – your investments should be able to grow at an average annual rate of 8.5 percent. In recent times, inflation in the United States has averaged about 3 percent a year. Simple math shows that your investments will generate 5.5 percent annually in income after you reinvest the 3 percent needed to keep up with inflation.

Here is a table that shows how much money you need to have invested by the time you retire in order to realize the perpetual income you desire. Now all you need to do is figure out how to squirrel away that much money during the years between now and then.

Regular income you need	Principal required to provide it
$1,000	$18,182
$5,000	$90,909
$10,000	$181,818
$20,000	$363,636
$50,000	$909,091
$100,000	$1,818,182

Furthermore, when you invest a regular amount each month, it costs you less annually than when you invest a regular amount only once a year. In addition, the earlier you start to invest for retirement – whether your asset allocation is for income, growth or some combination of the two – the less you will need to invest on a regular basis to reach your target amount. Here is an example using a goal of reaching a principal amount of $10,000 in 5, 15, and 30 years:

	Invest monthy	Invest yearly
5 years	$134 ($1,608 annually)	$1,688
15 years	$28 ($336 annually)	$354
30 years	$6 ($72 annually)	$81

In other words, save and invest early, and save and invest often.

A Good Handle on the Concept

Wendy, 35, thinks she can take income from her 401(k) plan once she is 59½ while the plan continues to grow. She is correct. Many other people have the false impression that their plan stops growing at this age. Nothing could be further from the truth. "I've never thought about it, but I would assume that my plan would still grow. I just won't be contributing to my plan, unless I write checks out of my own pocket." She has a good handle on this concept. She understands that when she retires, her account will need to continue growing in order to offset the effects of inflation.

Stephanie also understands the importance in retirement of being able to take out some money and continue having her portfolio grow. "Will that allocation be one-third for income and two-thirds for growth? I don't know," she says. She does know that her lifestyle and spending habits will not change much after she retires. "Since I won't be working *as much* – or *at all*, for that matter – I would like to travel more," she says. "However, I can't imagine I'll be spending six months traveling and six months at home."

She relocated recently from Michigan to Florida where she was raised, to take an executive job with GMAC. As a result, she has more time for leisure travel. Previously, the only time she traveled was to visit her parents in Florida. "Now that I'm home," she says, "I can go other places."

She is fortunate in another important way. She sold her house in an extremely depressed Detroit housing market for a small equity gain and is temporarily living with her parents until she buys a house in Florida. "I have no house bills," she says. "When I say that, I chuckle because part of me gets anxious and wants to go out and buy a house. The other part of me says the opposite: 'Are you stupid? Not that I'm a freeloader, but where in your life, at 40 years old, will you ever have an opportunity to save this type of money and still be with your parents?'" She does not worry about her present situation. "Whatever is going to happen, I'm sure I'll be fine," she says. With a self-effacing laugh, she adds, "I plan to have a child of my own and grow up again one day."

Stephanie is in great financial shape. Clearly, she does an excellent job of balancing her need for both income and growth when allocating her 401(k) plan's assets. She has a good idea of what she is doing, where she is going, and how she plans to get there. In short, she has a sound methodology.

Doing Exactly What She Needs to Do

Ann is young enough to seek growth rather than income from her 401(k) plan. This is exactly what she is doing. Indeed, she would love to live to 120. Based on her family's life expectancy, she will probably make it into her mid-80s. This raises an interesting question – one I addressed earlier (Chapter 1). How long do you expect to live in retirement? Only a handful of the people I interviewed for this book can produce a satisfactory response. Ann is not one of them. "I have no idea," she answers.

She does have, however, an idea of her life during her retirement years – however many they may be. In addition, it is a good one. "Certainly, I am going to plan so that my 401(k) will outlive me," she says. "I also don't think I will rely on just a 401(k) in retirement. I will have other investments outside the 401(k) as well. Even maxxing out a 401(k) for the next several years might not be enough. Hopefully, I'm going to have a lot of different places to draw money from in retirement."

Still, she is unsure whether she is now doing enough of the right things so that her retirement funds will outlive her. "It's hard to say; it's so early," she says. "I have so far to go before retirement and I've just started saving for it so recently." Without a doubt, she is young enough to affect completely the way she lives in retirement. This is because the next 25 to 30 years will likely be the biggest income-producing period of her working life. She needs to continue being fairly aggressive at saving money and relatively conservative at investing it for retirement. If she does this, she would be in good shape for her retirement years.

Amazingly, some of our clients in their late 50s or early 60s have under-saved. Now, they want us to *invest* aggressively their retirement money. We tell them to do the opposite: Become aggressive at *saving* their money for retirement and allow us to be relatively conservative at investing it.

Given her age, Ann is doing exactly what she needs to do. She is being aggressive at both saving and investing. She has $50,000 in retirement savings and "no problem" working until she is 70. "I would love to get $100,000 in my 401(k) by age 40," she says. "I feel that if I can do this and the money really does double very 10 years, I would be in decent shape by the time I'm 70." Even if Ann does not put another dime in her retirement plan between now and 70, her portfolio would probably be worth $800,000 when she reaches that age. Obviously, her portfolio would likely be worth several times more if she takes two actions: 1) Continues to save and invest aggressively for retirement; and 2) Not withdraw prematurely much if any money from her plan.

Many Storms and Good Times to Come

Omar, 34, has already told us (Chapter 4) that he has most of his retirement funds in stocks, which are volatile. He has done this because he does not plan to retire until he is in his 60s. "I have many storms to come!" he says. "And good times, too!" He figures correctly that he will have enough time to recover any losses his stock holdings may suffer over the next few years. He is young enough to take calculated risks with his retirement funds.

Valerie has also put more of her 401(k) money – 15 percent – in riskier investments than she will when she is much older. She has invested for the long term, figuring she will eventually recover any losses she suffers. I ask her what it means to balance her need for both income and growth when she allocates her plan's assets.

Like many people – both young and old – she struggles with the question. "I would take cash out of my retirement fund *while* using the fund to create more money?" she ponders. Yes, this is precisely what it means.

Many other people are quite surprised to learn their retirement money can continue to grow after they retire – even when they stop investing upon retirement. The key is, however, to avoid withdrawing annually more from your retirement fund than it grew by that year.

I understand why Valerie is hesitant about her ability – and need – to strike a balance between income and growth even in retirement. She is relatively young and, therefore, decades away from needing to address this issue. Eventually, though, she will need to decide whether to generate monthly cash flow from her retirement plan to pay for basic living expenses while allowing her portfolio to continue growing. If and when she makes this choice, she would need to become more conservative with her investments to accommodate this cash flow.

I find it odd and frustrating that too many of us believe our retirement funds will retire and stop growing altogether when we retire from or quit our jobs. Quite mistakenly, we think our portfolios will suddenly revert to generating only income for our immediate expenses and no growth for our future years.

While I have no clear idea where this erroneous notion comes from, it is very pervasive. One factor that may contribute to it is so-called "lifestyle funds" that are now on the market. They are targeted for use at the "age of retirement," which does not mean much. "Age of retirement" means only when you are no longer working a full-time job, and has nothing to do with the money you have saved and invested for retirement. Lifestyle funds send a false signal to people who may have a life expectancy of 35 or more years beyond when they retire.

He Gets It

No surprises from Andrew on this score. He gets it. Currently, he needs his plan to produce growth, not income. "I understand there is a higher risk involved with higher growth," he says. "I'm willing to take that risk right now. If I do make a mistake now, I would have time to make it up," he adds. "As I get older, I will plan for the income."

He is correct. Unless he strikes it rich and retires much earlier than the rest of us, he has more than three decades to go before retiring. When he does quit working, he expects to continue investing for growth. "I like the risky nature of it all," he says. He predicts, however, he will adjust his holdings toward the more conservative side. He figures it will be 60 percent for income and 40 percent for growth – nearly the opposite of now.

You might think this would be a risky approach for someone in retirement. I, however, view the methodology Andrew plans to use in his retirement years as conservative and reasonable because he quite probably will increase his portfolio's size over the long haul.

Wisdom Beyond Her Years

Jennifer understands well the need to allocate her retirement plan's assets to produce both income and growth. She opened her 401(k) plan two years ago and cites one of the beauties of starting a plan at a young age. "It gave me a lot more options as opposed to people who start later in life," she says. "I don't have to play catch-up."

Primarily, she relies on her 401(k) for growth, not income. The portfolio contains some holdings that produce dividends, though, which she immediately invests back into her plan. She also has two mutual funds outside her 401(k) plan. She uses one of them for income. It produces dividends, which she also reinvests right away in the fund. In addition, she relies on her other mutual fund for growth. "The No. 1 thing with balancing income and growth," she says, "is to look at where you are, what you have saved and when you want to retire."

Once again, she points us to Google as an excellent tool for general research on the best ways to strike a healthy balance between income and growth at each stage of our lives. In addition, she urges us to discuss this matter with a financial planner.

Jennifer displays wisdom beyond her years on yet another important retirement-planning issue. She again recommends (as she did in Chapter 6) that we reallocate and rebalance at least annually our plan's assets on a tactical basis. She goes beyond this, though. "You should do it even when you go through different stages in your life," she says. "Examples are when you get married, have kids, reach the next phase of your career and approach retirement. You need to step back and look at what you are doing in each one of those phases. What I am now doing at 28, I am not going to be doing, if it's risky, at 63, when I'm two years away from retirement. Retirement is stability and your funds need to reflect that."

While Jennifer has yet to get married or have children, she expects eventually to do both. As a result, she plans for retirement as though she will live forever so that her money will outlive her. (See Chapter 1 for more on this subject.) "Anything that is left over is going to be a gift to my children," she says. "I plan to have as much growth as possible so they don't have to take care of me in a nursing home."

Jennifer is unusual in this regard because she is very young and yet already planning for retirement. She has clearly put good thought into what she plans to do and how she intends to do it, and it is not only because she is well educated. I think all you need to do in this regard is to have your head screwed on right and think past next year.

CHAPTER 10 401(K)NOWLEDGE GAINS

- Adopt one of three types of retirement portfolios, based on how far from (or close to) needing cash flow from your plan that you are: aggressive growth; moderately aggressive growth; or fairly conservative growth.

- Generate a cash-flow figure to determine how much principal you will need to have invested for your retirement.

- Calculate how much net income your retirement investments will generate annually after factoring for inflation.

- Invest a regular amount each month, which costs less annually than investing a regular amount only once a year.

- Start earlier rather than later in life to invest for retirement, which will reduce the amount you need to invest on a regular basis to reach your target amount.

11

Borrow Judiciously From Your Plan- If at All

Mortgage your house, not your retirement.

I wish I could say we always have another option when we need cash, besides borrowing from our 401(k). The truth of the matter is, sometimes this might be our *only* choice. Whenever possible, we should borrow money from our 401(k) only as a last resort.

Having said this, I urge you to avoid as much as possible borrowing money from your retirement plan. As I wrote in *The Scarborough Plan: Maximizing the Power of Your 401(k)*, you will have to pay about the same interest as you would face with a commercial loan – interest that you cannot deduct from your income tax anyway. The loan term will probably be less favorable than what a bank would give you – the limit for full repayment would be five years on anything but a first-time purchase. Your bank will probably give you more time than that to repay a loan to buy a car or boat or to finance your child's education.

Besides your 401(k) being a bad loan source, borrowing from it is also a bad deal for your retirement. When you borrow money from your retirement account, the borrowed funds stop growing. You may think that all you are losing is additional interest the borrowed money would have earned for you had you kept it in the 401(k). However, you are also missing the chance to let the borrowed money continue earning dividends and capital gains for you, which can result in a serious long-term earnings loss. Furthermore – as if you need a "furthermore" – once you repay the loan with *after*-tax dollars, those dollars are taxed again when you start taking distributions from your plan during your retirement years. The only winner is Uncle Sam!

One final caveat: If you leave your current employment during the course of your loan repayment, the loan would usually be callable. This means the employer you are leaving could demand the immediate repayment of the balance of the loan. Therefore, if you need to borrow money, go to the bank and obtain a home-equity loan or line of credit. Do not mortgage your retirement funds!

How about using your 401(k) funds to buy a home? That is allowed, right? Yes, it is allowed, but it also may not be in your best interest for all the reasons I have mentioned, plus one more. The maximum home-purchase loan you will be able to take is $50,000 – assuming your 401(k) account contains at least $100,000 and you have no other outstanding loans. As I said before, go to the bank. Mortgage your house, not your retirement.

Greg, Neil, and Carol have taken loans from their retirement funds. Greg is comfortable with his decision. Neil and Carol are not. So far resisting the urge to use their 401(k) to finance purchases are Wendy, Andrew, Ann, Jennifer, Kim, and Omar. Carrie does not yet have a 401(k) plan, but insists she would borrow from one only if she truly had to. In Omar's case, he once needed to borrow money. He did so, however, in a way that helped him to avoid an onerous double tax.

Succumbed To Temptation

In the late 1980s, Greg took a loan from his 401(k) for home improvements. He and his wife decided against borrowing the money from a bank instead. "I felt more secure working with my own money," he says. He is much older and wiser now. Would he consider borrowing now from his retirement plan? "No," he responds. "Now, at this age, I don't see the need to borrow. But if I did, I would try to avoid borrowing from my plan. I would also seek advice from my financial advisor."

Neil also dislikes the idea of borrowing from his 401(k). Yet, he admits he has been "guilty of it on two different occasions." Once, he needed cash. "I repaid it quickly," he says. Another time, he bought a boat, which he owns to this day. "It's not a good thing to borrow money from your plan," he says. He points to the interest on the loan and cites the value and growth potential borrowed money loses because it is no longer working. Still, he feels good about the loan he took from his 401(k) to purchase the boat. When he and his wife divorced a few years ago, he got the boat!

Many people always avoid borrowing money from their 401(k).
Like Greg and Neil, Carol is not one of them. She once took a loan
from her plan to buy a car. Her rationale at the time: "If I have to
pay interest on a loan, I'd rather pay it to my 401(k) plan. Looking
back, I would never do that again, I don't really know if that cost
me money, or what long-term effects it had on my account. Right
now, I feel there's no way I want to touch my 401(k)." That is,
until she retires.

When she borrowed from her plan, she was much younger and
much further from retirement. "I thought it wasn't going to make
that much of a difference," she says. "I've always been curious to see
if it did make that much difference." I tell her she does not really
want to know. "Let's leave it at that!" she responds.

Carol describes herself as "a little older, a little wiser and a little
more educated on investments. I think I'm just a little more
astute as an investor now. It's best to let your money work for you.
Anytime you touch that money, you're losing."

She does admit, though, that she has fought an urge in recent years
to borrow from her plan to buy real estate. At the time, she figured
the property would increase in value more than her 401(k) would
over the same amount of time. "I don't even trust that anymore!"
she says. Still, she believes she would be justified in borrowing
money from her 401(k) to buy a primary or even a secondary
home. "This is completely different from – and much more
rational than – borrowing from the plan to invest speculatively
in real estate," she says.

You need to be extremely cautious about borrowing money from
your 401(k) plan. The reason is quite simple: You are borrowing
from the very money that you have set aside for your long-term
retirement. As a result, you need to think long and hard about
taking out this money before then for *any* reason! Having said
this, too many people more easily rationalize borrowing – than not
borrowing – money from their plan. They come up with all sorts of

scenarios as to why it makes sense to do so. At the end of the day, I tend to disagree with most of these situations.

Resisted the Temptation

Wendy adds another distinct voice to the "Never Borrow from Your Plan" choir. She has been tempted to do so on at least one occasion. "The sale of our condo fell through recently and the purchase of our new home was still proceeding," she says. "So I did think for a short time about how to get money for the down payment."

Federal law allows you to borrow up to 50 percent of your 401(k) to purchase a house. For a first-time home purchase, you get up to 15 years to repay the loan with interest. If it is *not* your first-time buy, your repayment period would be only up to five years. "We didn't have to go that route, thank God!" Wendy says. "I wouldn't want to have to pay back my 401(k), which is there for the long haul, for a short-term purchase."

Carrie, meanwhile, thanks her grandfather and herself for her ability to resist borrowing from her 401(k) once she has one. For her, it is simply a bad idea. "This is money set aide for my retirement," she says, "and I don't want to touch it." She is quick to acknowledge, though, that life sometimes requires us to make difficult, unpleasant decisions. "I know that if something were to arise and I needed the money, I might have to borrow from my plan," she says. "But that option would be way on the back burner."

I like to hear Wendy, Carrie and many other people express an intense dislike of ever borrowing from their retirement plan. I yearn to hear even more people voice this same opinion. I believe we are nearly always mistaken when we remove money from our 401(k) before we are 59½. Again, I recognize the exceptions born of necessity.

Wendy has a good grasp on this issue. The more people that act like her, the better off they will be. With Carrie's attitude and approach, she should be in great shape if she ever finds herself between a financial rock and a hard place. She could tap into her fund if truly necessary.

A Double Whammy

Andrew has never borrowed from his 401(k). However, he is not opposed to doing so. "The only time I ever would is if I lived in an emerging neighborhood, and I had an opportunity to upgrade into a house," he says. "I might use money from my 401(k) for a down payment on the house. Other than that, I wouldn't use it, unless I truly had to." He has an amazingly healthy approach to borrowing from his plan. He is quite unusual in this regard.

Ann has also yet to borrow from her 401(k). She does not plan to do so anytime soon. "It would have to be a serious personal or family-member health crisis. That would be it!" she says. "I would really try to avoid it at all costs because there could be a double tax whammy if you do that." She has a sizeable emergency fund for large, extraordinary, and necessary expenses. "Hopefully, this fund will be big enough to cover me for anything that comes up," she says.

Ann has a smart attitude and approach to borrowing from her plan. Again, I wish many more of us felt and acted the same way. Several years ago, I testified before Congress regarding 401(k) plans. Then as now, I believe our federal lawmakers should eliminate the loan provision in 401(k) plans. The legal ability to borrow from our plans does not fit well with our long-term financial needs for our retirement. Nevertheless, Congress has yet to see fit to change this law.

A Slippery Slope

Jennifer also opposes borrowing money from her 401(k) for anything but "the last resort." When she bought her house, she resisted a real estate broker's suggestion that she borrow from her plan to help finance the purchase. "I was like, 'You're out of your skull,'" she says. When necessary, she can borrow money from her parents. She can also stop investing funds in her money-market account. "There are a lot of different places you can go," she says.

She strongly dislikes the idea of borrowing from her plan because doing so could result in a penalty tax for early withdrawal. There are, however, occasions when you can borrow short-term and penalty-free from a plan. "But if you're doing it short-term and depending on your income, you could instead get that money from a money-market account or from turning off your cable TV for a while," she says. "When you borrow outside your means, I don't think you should borrow from your 401(k) plan. You may decide you don't need the house right now. Instead, you could extend your lease for a while and save up the money." She also recognizes that borrowing from a 401(k) is a bad idea even when no penalty tax applies. This is because the money we take as a loan stops earning interest in our plan.

Jennifer cites yet another good reason not to borrow from her retirement plan. "My money goes from my paycheck to my 401(k) before I ever see it," she says. "If I start to use that money, it would become another tool for me. I might say to myself, 'I borrowed once and it worked out. Now, I can do it a second time,'" she adds. "It's a slippery slope."

Indeed, it is a slippery slope. As I said in Carol's case, some people justify borrowing from their retirement plan because they did so once before and it worked out well for them. As a result, they figure it is going to work out well again and become comfortable with borrowing from their portfolio.

A Saver at Heart

Kim joins our chorus of people who have never taken a loan from their 401(k). Nor does she plan to do so. She has been able to adopt this strategy because she has non-401(k) investments, including a regular savings account. When necessary, she can use – and has used – this money to pay bills and other necessary living expenses. In the past year, she borrowed this money to retire her house mortgage.

She regards herself as a saver at heart. "In a way, I'm kind of lucky because I'm single and I have no kids, so basically my income is strictly for me. I have a tendency to save it. Then, when I really want to spend it on something, the money is there for me to use."

I say this somewhat tongue-in-cheek: Kim is proof positive that one good retirement strategy is to avoid getting married and having children. She lives in a nice house – one that is not a mansion. She also drives a nice car – but not a luxury vehicle. Unlike too many other people, she does not spend every dollar she makes. Instead, she saves a good portion of it. If anything, she is living *below* her means. If many more Americans behaved as Kim does, we would not have a savings-rate crisis in this country. It would be a far different and better world!

Omar: "Never Touch Your 401(k) for *Anything!*"

Omar has never even considered borrowing from his 401(k). He cites one of the rules he lives by: "Never touch your 401(k) for *anything!*" This is why he has money-market funds in a Roth IRA. He plans to use them for the down-payment on the house that he plans eventually to buy.

I encourage you to do everything possible to avoid touching your 401(k) before you retire. It makes no sense to borrow the funds on which you are planning your life in retirement. Let us say you borrow appropriately from your plan and, therefore, do not incur a penalty tax. The loan repayments you make will include interest charges.

However, tax law regards interest payments as taxable earnings to your plan. When you withdraw this interest amount from your plan upon reaching 59½, you must pay yet another tax on it. Therefore, you pay taxes *twice* on the same money. I regard this as an insidious tax. I also find that most people are unaware of it.

Over these 11 chapters, I have shared with you numerous, valuable pieces of 401(k)nowledge culled from a quarter-century of experience on the financial-investment front lines. In addition, 20 other people agreed graciously to share with you the good, the bad, and the ugly of their 401(k) experiences. The lessons you can take away from this book boil essentially down to the titles of its 11 chapters:

1. What does planning for and living in retirement mean to you?
2. Participate actively in the makeup of your 401(k) plan.
3. Determine your investor profile.
4. Allocate your plan's assets appropriately.
5. Limit your plan's exposure to company stock.
6. Reallocate and rebalance your plan's assets on a tactical basis.
7. Do not panic when the value of your plan declines.
8. Know your plan's options and features.
9. Consider the tax consequences of your actions regarding your plan.
10. Balance your need for both income and growth when allocating your plan's assets.
11. Borrow judiciously from your plan – *if* at all.

I am always curious to find out how people think about the way they will spend their money in retirement. Their attitude speaks volumes about how they will likely manage and take distributions of their money. Here is a pair of philosophical questions, which I argue are the most important financial ones you will need to answer regarding your retirement:

- Do you intend just to live off the interest produced by your retirement portfolio?
- Do you expect your portfolio to continue growing while also producing cash flow on which you can live?

I do not think most people answer these questions well prior to retirement. They might intuitively have some ideas about them, but they have truly not thought them out. I hope that *401(k)nowledge: Practical Advice for Retiring on Your Own Terms* will help you to avoid this dismal fate of being unprepared for retirement. I wish you all a financially secure lifestyle in your golden years.

CHAPTER 11 401(K)NOWLEDGE GAINS

- When borrowing money, look first to obtain a home-equity loan or line of credit from a bank instead of mortgaging your retirement funds.

- When borrowing money from your retirement account, the lent funds stop earning interest, dividends and capital gains, which can result in a serious long-term earnings loss.

- When borrowing from your 401(k) to buy a home, you can use up to 50 percent of your retirement account the house. As a first-time homebuyer, have up to 15 years to repay the loan with interest. Otherwise, it is only up to five years.

- When making loan repayments to your 401(k) plan, the interest portion is a taxable earning to your retirement account. When you withdraw this interest amount from your plan upon reaching 59½, you must pay yet another tax on it.

Epilogue

The clients I fired – and
why I got rid of them.

At Scarborough Capital Management, we fire one of every 100 of our clients. There is a good reason for such a small number. By the time they hire us to manage their 401(k)s, they are scared to death! I am not, however, going to name names here.

My purpose for this epilogue is to **boldface**, *italicize,* and <u>underline</u> the fact that our 401(k)s are not trading, get-rich-quick or fun-money accounts. They are repositories of our serious, long-term retirement money. The clients we fire are those who ask us to day-trade their 401(k)s. They want to guess what the next hot market is or they want us to take a stab at it. The problem is not that they refuse to hear what we say to them; it is that they fail to listen to and understand enough of our advice.

I refuse to be part of a debacle. Therefore, we tell these clients, "You're not listening. We know what we are doing. Frankly, you're wasting $365 a year by paying us to do what *you* think is best." Usually, these clients' retirement portfolios are doing well. That is, until they ask us to start flipping their money. This is when we fire them. Some of these former clients try subsequently to return to us. We never take them back.

In 2001, a client fired *us*! Back then, the stock market was absolutely tanking. Yet she cancelled our services at the end of the year because we had failed to produce at least a 10 percent annual return for her. She said, "I'm paying you to manage my money to make me 10 percent or more a year." She was acting irrationally.

Typically, about 10 percent of our clients fire us. They then try to self-manage their 401(k)s. About half of them fail to do so and rehire us several months or years later. "This is a lot tougher than I ever thought it would be," they tell us upon returning. "Thank goodness you are again managing my 401(k) for me."

With this in mind, I offer five ways to avoid our firing you:

1. Do not get giddy when the market goes up.
2. Do not panic when it goes down.
3. Do not look at your account every day.
4. Keep saving and investing money for retirement.
5. Let us manage the retirement money for you.

How well do I follow my own advice? Quite well! I put 20 percent of my paycheck into a 401(k) and let the director of our research department manage my account. I do not even look at it very often. Indeed, I cannot tell you within $20,000 how much money it contains. And no, my 401(k) manager has never threatened to fire me as a client!